Victoria,

It's great fun to
with you. Thanks for all
your help.

[signature]

5/29/14

Winning

with

Liquid
Alternatives

Norman E. Mains, Phd

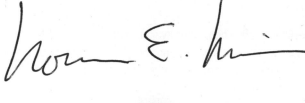

New York   Chicago   San Francisco   Athens   London   Madrid
Mexico City   Milan   New Delhi   Singapore   Sydney   Toronto

1 2 3 4 5 6 7 8 9 0   DOC/DOC   1 0 9 8 7 6 5 4

ISBN   978-0-07-183069-0
MHID   0-07-183069-3

e-ISBN   978-0-07-183070-6
e-MHID   0-07-183070-7

Library of Congress Cataloging-in-Publication Data

Mains, Norman.
  Winning with liquid alternatives : how to achieve your financial goals by investing in '40 Act alternative mutual funds / by Norman Mains.
     pages cm
  ISBN 978-0-07-183069-0 (hardback) — ISBN 0-07-183069-3 (hardback)
1. Mutual funds. 2. Hedge funds. 3. Asset allocation. 4. Portfolio management. I. Title.
  HG4530.M24 2014
  332.63'27—dc23   2014001657

McGraw-Hill Education books are available at special quantity discounts to use as premiums and sales promotions or for use in corporate training programs. To contact a representative, please visit the Contact Us pages at www.mhprofessional.com.

To my wife, Ginna

Contents

Preface

When I was approached to submit an outline to McGraw-Hill for a book, I'll admit that I was a little intimidated. However, after giving the subject a little thought, I realized that my topic, the rise of Liquid, or Investment Company Act of 1940 ('40 Act) Alternatives, had mostly occurred during my career in financial markets. Moreover, my various professional positions had given me a somewhat unique vantage point on their creation as one of the most important developments in contemporary financial history. So let's begin at the beginning.

After studying economics as an undergraduate at the University of Colorado in Boulder, I applied to the same school for a PhD program in economics. In hindsight, this was not a very good choice. I earned an MA degree after one year, maintaining nearly straight A's in my classes. Unfortunately, I wasn't really learning very much. I was taking graduate-level courses taught by the same professors I had had as an undergraduate. Sure, the reading lists were longer, but the professors didn't have that much new material in their graduate classes.

About midway through my second year, I got a lucky break. A visiting professor who liked my work was about to take an endowed chair at the University of Warwick in Warwickshire, England, and he offered to arrange a grant for me if I matriculated into the PhD program there.

Having never been to Europe, I saw this as a great opportunity. I returned to the United States a couple of years later with a good PhD thesis topic but very little actually done on writing the dissertation. Needing a job, I was put in touch with the Securities and Exchange Commission's (SEC's) chief economist, who interviewed me for a position on the team assigned to the soon-to-be-underway Institutional Investor Study. Unfortunately, it was a civil service position, so it was going to take about six months to actually get me hired. I was broke, and I needed a job. The SEC's chief economist was kind enough to call the chief economist at the mutual fund industry's trade association, the Investment Company Institute (ICI), because he knew that the ICI was looking for an associate economist.

The ICI was a perfect fit for me because my thesis topic was focused on whether mutual fund portfolio managers could augment their investment returns by shifting the "riskiness" of their portfolios to enhance their investment returns. It is now, by the way, an almost forgotten fact that virtually all the early work in risk measurement and performance management in financial markets was based on the investment results of mutual funds. Why? Because mutual funds published their net asset values on a daily basis, and researchers could build a databases that largely encompassed the industry. Academicians and other researchers could then test various hypotheses via statistical methods on the early computer systems. My thesis convinced me and my external readers at the Wharton School of Business that mutual fund portfolio managers were not very good at predicting overall market swings, but they were much better at identifying undervalued and overvalued equities.

Having completed my PhD thesis, I was then fortunate to be offered a job as a research economist at the Federal Reserve Board in Washington, DC. Rather than focusing on equities, however, the Fed's director of research asked me to become the board's senior researcher on the corporate and municipal bond markets. When I protested to him that I really didn't know very much about fixed income, he simply responded, "Don't worry, you'll learn."

Almost seven years later, I was a senior economist in the Fed's U.S. Treasury and agency market when I received an unsolicited telephone call from the individual who created the interest rate futures market at the Chicago Board of Trade (CBOT). He was in the process of organizing a new group at a firm he had just joined, Drexel Burnham Lambert (DBL), and he asked me if I would be interested in creating a research team for DBL's institutional financial futures and options group? It was a big jump to go from the cloistered halls of the

Federal Reserve Board to the open-outcry futures markets in Chicago, but financial futures, and later options on futures, were still in their infancy. These financial instruments were not called derivatives in the 1980s but eventually would become one of the major financial markets, not just in the United States, but around the globe.

Toward the end of my tenure at DBL, my group launched one of the earliest alternative investment products, a managed futures fund. It was momentum-based strategy managed by a very well known and successful "pit" trader. These types of managed funds were known as *commodity trading advisors* (CTAs), and they were not widely known at the time. It took my group and the vaunted DBL sales force nearly a year to raise the initial fund, which started trading in January 1987 with total net assets of $40 million. The portfolio manager (PM) was famous for turning his initial stake of a few thousand dollars into more than $100 million, and the fund's initial results were spectacular. After only two months, the fund was up about 18 percent, and we couldn't get a second fund registered and sold quickly enough. We launched the second fund, this time with $100 million of net assets, in June 1987. Both funds were traded in a very similar fashion, and the early strong results of fund number one were completely retraced, and fund number two had sizable early losses. By the time Labor Day arrived, both funds were below their initial offering prices.

Students of financial history will recall that Alan Greenspan became chairman of the Federal Reserve Board in August 1987, and he promptly raised the Federal Reserve's discount rate over the Labor Day weekend. The portfolio manager of the two DBL funds elected to go heavily "short" in Eurodollar futures following the announcement because increases in short-term interest rates by the Federal Reserve are usually followed by additional changes in the same direction. Financial markets and stock prices gyrated wildly over the next two months, and U.S stock prices eventually fell by a record amount for a single day, Black Monday, when the Dow Jones Industrial Average (DJIA) dropped by 508 index points, or 22.61 percent. In response to these market conditions, the Federal Reserve issued on the next day a press release essentially stating that it would "do what was necessary" to ensure the integrity of financial markets around the world. Market participants took this as meaning that the Fed would flood the markets with liquidity, and short-term interest rates recorded one of their largest one-day declines in modern history on the Tuesday following the record decline in the DJIA. This was not good news for DBL's two CTA funds. The operating agreements of both funds had provisions that called for the cessation of trading by each fund if its value dropped to one-half the initial offering price, and this is exactly what happened. Shareholders in the funds were, not surprisingly, quite upset, and it proved to be a lasting lesson for me that financial market outcomes can be highly unpredictable, and therefore, adequate risk control is paramount.

I moved on from DBL about a year later, first running an equity-oriented research department for a Los Angeles–based financial services firm and then returning to Chicago, where I was president and chief administrative officer of a regional broker-dealer with, among other activities, a sizable commodities division. When that firm was taken over by a Mexican-based financial services firm, I became chief economist and director of research of the Chicago Mercantile Exchange. This was the early to middle 1990s, and hedge funds were beginning to have an impact because they were amassing net assets at a very fast pace. Next, I commuted to Princeton, New Jersey, for a few months while I was affiliated with Dow Jones Indexes, but I eventually was offered the position of president of one of the money management arms of a large French bank that had a futures and options clearing subsidiary in Chicago. The group initially created funds of CTA fund products for international clients. The group started in the late 1980s, but by the mid-1990s, the clients were more interested in hedge funds than CTAs, so the focus was on creating funds of hedge funds.

One of the more innovational aspects of my team's offering was to allow ultra-high-net-worth customers to pick their own mix of hedge funds and CTAs from a select list of vehicles that my team had subjected to rigorous due diligence. This gave my team the opportunity to convey to clients and potential clients that return and volatility were inadequate measures of judgment but that the cross-correlations of investment management vehicles with each other were equally important.

After a few years at that firm, I got an opportunity to become the director of research and chief investment officer of Graystone Partners. Graystone was a firm that was started by three individuals in Chicago that focused on the investment needs of ultra-high-net-worth individuals and family offices. It was especially well known for its expertise in allocating to hedge funds in the early to middle 1990s. Morgan Stanley acquired Graystone at the beginning of 2000, and I joined the group in the spring of 2001. Once I joined the group, I was surprised to learn that its due diligence process was viewed by senior Morgan Stanley management as being too thin. Moreover, the group's process for selecting hedge funds was not very scientific (a trait shared by most fund of hedge fund organizations at the time), although Graystone's was known for customizing fund of hedge funds for ultra-high-net-worth individuals and family offices.

What does customization mean? Most wealthy individuals have a core source of wealth, such as real estate or an exploration and production energy company. As such, these individuals typically have a very high proportion of their wealth tied up in the core activity. Most fund of hedge funds are broadly diversified against as many potential risks as possible. But, if an individual already has a large exposure to, say, energy, then he or she probably would want to avoid an equity long/short hedge fund that has a persistent long exposure to energy. Graystone specialized in designing customized funds of hedge funds that took into account the wealthy individual's core holdings.

The other notable contribution of Graystone Research was my team's creation of the first factor model that identified the sources of return and risk for hedge fund substrategies and then assembled funds of funds by matching the characteristics of the investor's requirements in a mathematical routine that optimized the appropriate mix of hedge funds to fit the return requirements and risk tolerance of the client. This is a technique that has been copied and modified by various hedge fund service providers, but it was highly innovational when my team introduced it in 2002.

Most of Graystone's clients were brought to the team by Morgan Stanley's private wealth management (PWM) investment advisors. Many of these PWM clients have investable assets of at least $20 million, although the typical Graystone client had investable assets of at least $50 million. The clients' assets were very high because it seemed reasonable to have 20 percent of the clients' wealth in hedge funds. Moreover, my group's research showed that a well-diversified fund of hedge fund portfolio needed at least 10 hedge funds to meet this objective. Hedge funds, as you will learn later in this book, are restricted to the number of clients that can be investors. As a result, most hedge funds have a minimum investment requirement of at least $1 million, so a well-diversified fund of hedge funds would need to be about $10 million and this requires total investable assets of $50 million for the 20 percent allocation rule.

The United States is by almost every measure a very wealthy country. Nevertheless, when I was with Graystone Research, I was always amazed at how many PWM clients had investable assets of $20 million and even $50 million. At the same time, when I would study surveys of investable wealth, the number of potential clients with $20 million was always amazing to me. Even more amazing, however, was the number of investors with investable assets of, say, $500,000 to $20 million. This group is popularly called the *mass affluent*, and their numbers simply dwarf the number of ultra-high-net-worth investors. What is it that ultra-high-net-worth investors are seeking in allocating to hedge funds? The answer is straightforward: acceptably high returns with risk controls that moderate losses when markets decline. But why should these types of investments be limited to the wealthiest investors? They shouldn't.

This brings me to my current position. When I resigned from Morgan Stanley, I joined Forward, an investment management company that focuses primarily on mutual funds and, to a lesser degree, on separately managed accounts and hedge funds. Forward is not your typical investment management company. Forward specializes in offering investment products that use the techniques and strategies employed by hedge funds, but offering these products with daily liquidity, high transparency, and the regulatory regime of mutual funds. Mutual funds are regulated by the SEC, based, initially, on the Investment Company Act of 1940 ('40 Act). Thus, these vehicles are called *'40 Act alternative mutual funds* or just *'40 Act alternatives*. Another popular name for these vehicles is *liquid alternatives*, where the term *liquid* is used to emphasize that investors can liquidate (and buy) the funds on a daily basis. Throughout this book, I will use *'40 Act alternatives* and *liquid alternatives* interchangeably.

This book will attempt to convey the attributes and limitations of these '40 Act alternative vehicles. Hedge fund total net assets are currently more than $2.0 trillion, but relatively few investors are able to qualify for them. '40 Act alternatives are just beginning to grow. This book will hopefully introduce you to the attributes of these liquid alternative vehicles, and this knowledge will help you to use these vehicles in your portfolio. Ideally, this knowledge will allow you to achieve your financial goals in a more efficient manner going forward.

I started my professional career with ICI. I then spent several years with various firms that touched on fixed income, futures, options, derivatives, indexes, hedge funds, and other seemingly esoteric investment vehicles. My current firm isn't the largest mutual fund management company, but we consider ourselves to be among the *thought leaders* in the industry. I hope that you will agree with this assessment when you finish this book.

Acknowledgments

As a member of the senior management team at Forward, I must begin my acknowledgments by recognizing all my fellow workers at Forward for giving me the opportunity to conceive and complete this work. In particular, Forward's chief executive officer, Alan Reid, has been very supportive of the project, and he was always willing to make resources available to me, both from within and outside the firm, to contribute to the project. I benefited from interacting with several members of the Forward senior management team (Clay Smudsky, Rob Naka, Jim O'Donnell, Loire White, Judy Rosenberg, Jeff Cusack, and Paul Schaefer) on many aspects of the mutual fund industry that are covered in this book. In addition, the firm's Strategic Information group played an important role in assisting me with many of the calculations and analyses in the book. I especially would like to cite Lance J. White for his yeoman's effort on my behalf, as well as Preeti Malik and Claire Ianiro for their efforts on the project. Steve Unzicker and Brigitte LeBlanc, independent contractors to Forward, were also very helpful. I have also benefited greatly from the editorial team assigned to me at McGraw-Hill, in particular Mary Glenn, Cheryl Ringer, and Daina Penikas. As much as I appreciate the help of all of these individuals, I must take full responsibility for any errors in the document.

1

Liquid Alternatives:
A New Breed Emerges

As with most revolutions, few people noticed it happening. Instead, most investors were focused on the roller-coaster ride of stock prices from the late 1990s through the first decade of the new millennium, the steady rise in fixed-income prices over the same span, and then the eventual meltdown of most asset prices in the "great recession" of 2008. The movement in asset values, or *price action*, over the period was probably the most significant development that captured the attention of investors. However, other significant developments were the rise of emerging markets, especially China, and the phenomenal growth of hedge funds and other alternative investment vehicles.

It wasn't until global financial markets posted their worst results since the 1930s that Investment Company Act of 1940 ('40 Act) alternative mutual funds truly began to capture the interest of the investing public. Hedge funds were, until the 2008 debacle, the darlings of the ultra-high-net-worth investing crowd. This erudite group of very well off individuals, family offices, endowments, and foundations had been dominating the financial media for over a decade. These investors and their advisors had been touting hedge funds, private equity, venture capital, and other alternative investments as a new paradigm. Their investment results seemed to be spectacular, but the overwhelming majority of U.S. and non-U.S. investors were statutorily barred from accessing these investment vehicles.

Early Stirrings of Liquid Alternatives

Very few people paid notice to the rise of '40 Act alternative mutual funds. These liquid alternatives began to gain momentum in the early part of the twenty-first century. The "great recession" was the real watershed. Investment tenets that were the backbone of investing for the previous three decades were called into question when investors saw their carefully constructed portfolios tumble in value. As all types of investors looked for answers, the hedge fund industry and its focus on absolute returns and risk control began to look better and better.

Alternative-investment mutual funds are, quite simply, mutual funds whose portfolio managers employ hedge fund strategies. But the very early days of these *hybrid* investment companies occurred when the hedge fund industry was just beginning to become a force in the financial marketplace. To fully understand what was happening, one needs to look at the early days of both mutual funds and hedge funds for clues to the allure of these vehicles.

Figure 1-1 illustrates that only four '40 Act alternative investment mutual funds were operating as of December 31, 1985, and these vehicles had total net assets of only $122.0 million. All four of these funds are still operating, although they have undergone some changes. Two of the mutual funds are engaged in option-writing strategies aimed at investment objectives of achieving return and managing risk with equity options. The earliest began operation on December 7, 1977, whereas the second began on July 8, 1978. The third is classified as a *bear market fund*. This means that it seeks total returns by usually having the portfolio's net exposure be negative, and it began operating on October 10, 1985. The fourth fund is a nontraditional bond fund, where the portfolio manager seeks to generate a positive absolute return through a combination of income and capital appreciation. To achieve this goal, the fund employs a total return strategy using investments in fixed-income securities that focus on income, appreciation, and capital preservation.

Understanding Net Asset Value

It's reasonable to wonder why the term *net asset value* is used with mutual funds rather than *asset value*. Net asset value (NAV) is the value of a fund's

FIGURE 1-1 '40 Act alternative mutual funds (dollar amounts in millions)

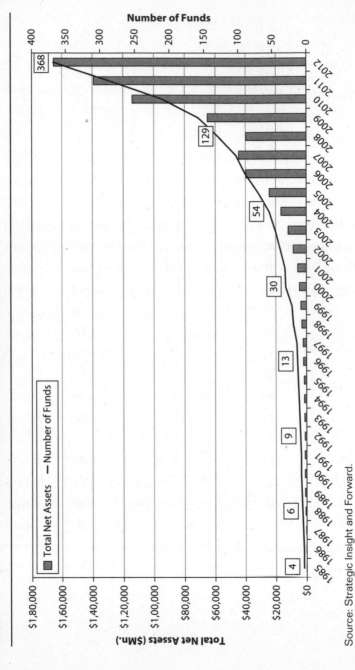

Source: Strategic Insight and Forward.

assets minus the value of its liabilities. In the case of '40 Act mutual funds, each fund posts a net asset value per share shortly after the 4 p.m. (Eastern time) closing of the New York Stock Exchange (NYSE). Net assets are the value of the mutual fund's portfolio of security holdings and cash at the time of the close minus the value of the fund's liabilities for the day. These liabilities reflect the fund's operating expenses such as management fees, transfer-agent fees, custodian fees, and other expenses. As an approximation, these fees average about 1 percent per year for many mutual funds. The *net asset value per share* price is the total net assets divided by the number of shares outstanding. The fund *strikes* a daily net asset value per share as of the close of the NYSE, and this is the price at which new shares are purchased and redeemed shares are sold.

The daily net asset value per share is a key statistic for computing performance. A mutual fund's one-year performance can be calculated by dividing the end-of-year net asset value plus any dividends per share and capital gains per share that were paid to shareholders during the year by the previous year's net asset value. Assume, for example, that a mutual fund's year-end net asset value was $10.80 per share and that its net asset value one year earlier was $10.00. Also assume that the fund distributed $0.05 in dividends and $0.15 in capital gains during the year. To calculate the annual performance, add the dividends per share and the capital gains per share to the year-end NAV per share, and divide by the previous year-end NAV per share ($10.80 + 0.05 + 0.15/$10.00) = $11.00/$10.00 = 1.10, or performance of 10 percent for the year.

A Brief History of Investment Companies

To grasp the history of '40 Act alternative mutual funds, it's useful to briefly describe the history of U.S. investment companies. They first became popular during the bull market of the 1920s, although their first incarnation was as investment trusts in Great Britain in the latter part of the nineteenth century. Many of the U.S. investment companies that started in the 1920s were closed-end funds that could trade in the open market at prices above or below the NAV of the fund's underlying portfolio. Moreover, the vehicles were able to issue *senior* securities to their common shares (such as preferred stock), and this is the functional equivalent of allowing them to use leverage. Other activities, such as self-dealing, also created a sordid atmosphere that thrived when overall stock prices were rising but produced higher losses when prices fell. The magnitude of the rise and fall of stock market prices is illustrated in Figure 1-2. The top line shows that stock prices, as measured by the Standard & Poor's 500 Stock Index (S&P 500), earned an average annual rate of return of 9.85 percent (including reinvesting all dividends) over the 87-year span between January 1, 1926 (the initiation of the index), and December 31,

FIGURE 1-2   Average annual rates of return and volatility for the S&P 500 for selected periods (percentages)

Period	Number of Years	Average Annual Rate of Return	Average Annual Standard Deviation
1/1/1926 through 12/31/2012	87	9.85	19.06
1/1/1926 through 12/31/1929	4	19.19	19.62
1/1/1930 through 12/31/1939	10	(0.05)	37.67
1/1/1940 through 12/31/1949	10	9.17	15.83
1/1/1950 through 12/31/1959	10	19.35	11.79
1/1/1960 through 12/31/1969	10	7.81	12.10
1/1/1970 through 12/31/1979	10	5.87	15.94
1/1/1980 through 12/31/1989	10	17.55	16.32
1/1/1990 through 12/31/1999	10	18.21	13.38
1/1/2000 through 12/31/2009	10	(0.95)	16.07
1/1/2010 through 12/31/2012	3	10.87	15.09

Source: Morningstar and Forward.

2012, and the average annual volatility over this span was 19.06 percent. However, stock prices rose by 19.19 percent over the four-year period that ended the "roaring twenties" on December 31, 1929, and stock price volatility was 19.62 percent. Most of the original group of U.S. investment companies, the closed-end funds, showed stellar performance over this period, but this was heavily due to their use of leverage.

Volatility and Risk

The widespread introduction of computers and high-speed data processing in the 1960s allowed researchers to process large volumes of data over increasingly shorter periods of time. Time-series analysis had always been important in economic analysis and financial markets, but the advent of computers greatly expanded the tools available to conduct research. As researchers turned their focus to stock price time series, they began to associate the dispersion of the prices over time as a measure of risk. In other words, *volatility* refers to the amount of uncertainty (or risk) around the level of a security's price. A high volatility (measured historically over some period) means that the price of a security can be expected to vary widely, both up or down, whereas a low volatility means that the future prices are unlikely to change much from their current levels. With a time-series analysis of prices for a security, the volatility can be measured statistically, and this is equated to risk. There are, of course, a number of ways to describe risk, but the variance or its standard deviation of prices is widely used in empirical studies.

The downside of this leverage became apparent, however, in the "great crash" of U.S. stock prices on October 29, 1929. In all, the slide of stock prices, as measured by the Dow Jones Industrial Average (DJIA), was –89.19 percent from its then-peak of 381.17 points on September 3, 1929, to its low of 41.22 points on July 7, 1932. The entire decade of the 1930s is now widely regarded as the Great Depression in the United States, and Figure 1-2 shows that stock prices posted a negative average annual rate of return of –0.05 percent over the 10 years while stock price volatility soared to an annual average of 37.67 percent. The enormous movement in stock prices, coupled with other events, eventually motivated the U.S. Congress to enact several new statutes, such as the Securities Act of 1933 and the Securities Exchange Act of 1934, that are the bedrock of U.S. securities market regulation.

The first mutual funds were created in Boston in 1924.[1] Unlike closed-end funds, they were designed to trade only at the underlying value of the portfolio's assets, and they were structured to constantly issue new shares to purchasers on a daily basis and stand ready to redeem, also on a daily basis, outstanding shares from existing shareholders deciding to liquidate. Mutual fund share values declined sharply over the 1929–1932 period, but unlike many of the closed-end funds, most of the early mutual funds survived and eventually began to gain total net assets. The mutual fund industry's trade association, the Investment Company Institute, states that 68 mutual funds were in existence on December 31, 1940, and these vehicles had total net assets of $0.5 billion. Figure 1-2 also shows that U.S. stock price returns began to improve in the 1940s; in fact, the S&P 500 returned, on average, 9.17 percent per year, and volatility calmed to 15.83 percent.

Hedge Funds Enter the Game

The early years of hedge funds also went unnoticed by the great majority of financial market participants. This was an era when now-commonplace terms such as *global macro*, *equity long/short*, and *relative-value arbitrage* were largely greeted with blank stares by most investors. Most hedge fund historians date their lineage to Alfred Winslow Jones, who started his first "hedged" fund in 1949.[2] It was an equity vehicle that could go both long securities and short securities so that the fund's net exposure could be positive or negative.

Prior to starting the investment company, Jones was a writer for *Fortune* magazine, and he was writing a story on technical trading strategies (i.e., identifying assets with positive or negative price momentum using nothing other than the asset's price history).[3] Two months before his *Fortune* article was published, Jones launched an investment partnership that spawned the hedge fund industry. Jones employed a lot of features in his hedge fund that are now commonplace. For example, it didn't completely rely on a rising stock market to generate gains for investors by being both long and short individual company stocks; it had the ability to use leverage to augment returns; it avoided registering under the Investment Company Act of 1940 by limiting the number of investors no more than 99; a sizable amount of the partnership's capital was Jones' own money; and the vehicle's management company had a fee schedule that paid it an annual fee of 2 percent plus a performance fee of 20 percent of profits.

Professional money management was still in its infancy when Jones started his hedge fund. According to the Investment Company Institute (ICI), there were 73 mutual funds in existence at year-end 1945, and these vehicles had total net assets of $1.3 billion or an average of only $17.8 million per mutual fund. The mutual fund industry starting growing rapidly in the post–World War II era, however, largely reflecting the relatively strong rise in stock prices plus the newly discovered propensity that allowed Americans to buy equities either directly or through vehicles offering professional money management.[4]

Mutual Funds Become a Force in the Marketplace

The 15-year period immediately following World War II witnessed an explosion in the growth of assets in mutual funds and the number of shareholders. The industry's *assets under management* (AUM) totaled $17.0 billion at the end of 1960, and the number of mutual funds had climbed to 171. Moreover, the number of shareholder accounts was 4.9 million.[5] This was a period, of course, when U.S. stock prices began to produce respectable returns with moderate volatility. Figure 1-2 shows, for example, that U.S. stock prices, as measured by the S&P 500, climbed 19.35 percent per year in the 1950s while average annual volatility declined to 11.79 percent.

Although most people associate mutual funds with the equity market, mutual fund managers can, of course, focus their investment holdings on a wide variety of financial

FIGURE 1-3   Asset composition of the U.S. mutual fund industry (dollar amount in billions, year-end)

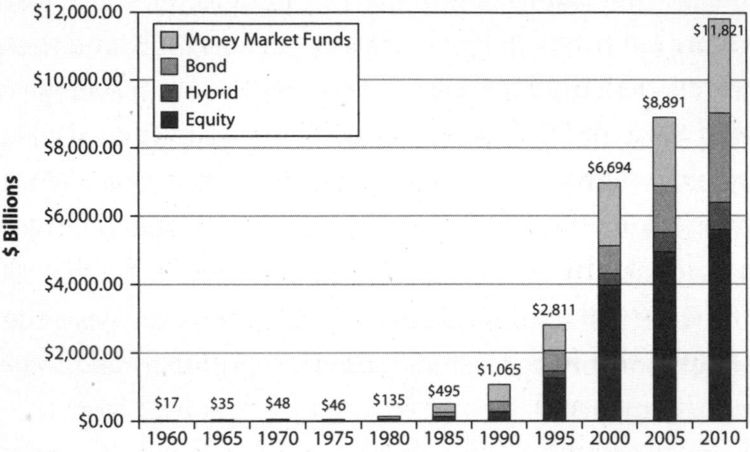

Source: Investment Company Institute Fact Book: 2012 and Forward.

assets. And, as the mutual fund industry grew in size, it also became much more diverse. Not only were holdings of traditional mutual funds expanded, but Figure 1-3 shows that new categories of mutual funds, such as money-market funds, debuted in 1971. This greatly expanded the scope and attractiveness of the industry. As time passed, U.S. Treasury, corporate, and, in 1976, municipal bond funds flourished and began attracting flows from investors seeking to diversify their investable assets.

As U.S. equity prices rose to then-unprecedented heights in the latter part of the 1960s, a 1968 survey by the Securities and Exchange Commission (SEC) estimated that 215 investment partnerships existed and that 140 of these were hedge funds. Many of these hedge fund portfolio managers were relying on leverage to boost their overall returns, and this, in turn, left them vulnerable to a market downturn. U.S. equity prices did move, in fact, sharply lower in late 1969 and early 1970. This drawdown was reversed in 1971 through 1973, but a new and deeper downward movement spanned the mid-1973 through mid-1975 period. In all, U.S. equity prices registered an average annual gain of only 5.87 percent in the 1970s (see Figure 1-2). This was, apparently, a particularly difficult period for the still-fledgling hedge fund industry. For example, the Jones vehicle, after outperforming broad stock indexes and highly regarded mutual funds, reportedly declined more than 35 percent in its fiscal year ending May 31, 1970, and the assets under management of the 28 largest hedge funds declined by 70 percent for the 1970 calendar year.[6] Many of the hedge funds were liquidated, and the remaining funds were estimated to have assets under management of only $300 million at year-end.

Other Early Pioneers of Hedge Funds

Very little was heard about hedge funds over the next 10 years or so, but a core group of portfolio managers continued to hone their investment skills and broaden their investment horizons. Early adopters of the hedge fund style of management were now-famous investors such as George Soros, Michael Steinhardt,[7] and Warren Buffett. Buffett started several investment partnerships in the 1950s and once worked for Benjamin Graham, the individual who coauthored an iconic book on value investing with David Dodd. Buffett eventually combined the partnerships into a single hedge fund and then dissolved it when he began using Berkshire Hathaway to invest in individual companies.

Many of these early hedge fund pioneers began adopting a more varied style of investing than just the equity long/short approach. Many hedge fund managers began trading actively in foreign exchange, commodity futures, and fixed-income markets, employing a "go-anywhere" approach. The financial press began calling these hedge vehicles *global macro funds*, but this eventually became a misnomer. Today, global macro hedge funds typically focus on simultaneously investing both long and short in equities and fixed-income, foreign-exchange, and commodity markets based on a view of global and regional relative values and price movements. George Soros and certain other hedge fund managers were employing a multistrategy approach that emphasized shifting the strategy weights to focus on the most attractive area or areas on a monthly or quarterly basis.[8]

Understanding Leverage and Risk

Leverage is an elusive term that means different things to different people. Leverage in financial markets is generally associated with potentially higher returns and losses, so there is a direct correspondence between leverage and risk. Investment companies in the 1920s, such as closed-end funds, were able to issue senior securities that had a higher preference for receiving interest or dividend payments, such as bonds and preferred stock. This leverage worked in favor of the common shareholders of closed-end funds when stock prices were rising, but it became a difficult issue when stock prices tumbled.

After the great crash of 1929, congressional hearings and studies concluded that the leverage of closed-end investment companies was a major cause of the precipitous decline in stock prices. The Securities Act of 1933 and the Securities and Exchange Act of 1934 were enacted in part to create a level playing field for individuals and institutions transacting in financial markets. Investment companies eventually were brought under the regulatory tent when the U.S. Congress enacted the Investment Company Act of 1940. With regard to leverage, the '40 Act initially prohibited closed- and open-end investment companies from issuing any senior securities.

This did not present a problem for mutual funds because these investment vehicles have, by design, only one class of shares—common stock. Closed-end funds argued, on the other hand, that an outright ban was overkill. As a result, Section 18 of the '40 Act limited leverage by requiring any issuer of bonds to have asset coverage of at least 300 percent and preferred stock to have asset coverage of at least 200 percent. Section 18 prohibited mutual funds from issuing senior securities and limited bank borrowings to those with asset coverage of at least 300 percent of liabilities. Liabilities include both borrowing to fund leveraged long positions and borrowed stock to fund short sales.

In the case of '40 Act vehicles, assume that a mutual fund has $100 million of long securities and no debt, so the fund would be 100 percent gross long. If the portfolio manager elected to short securities, he or she could do so up to $50 million because the borrowing would give the fund a gross exposure of 150 percent and a short, or borrowed, position of $50 million, or 33.3 percent. In this case, the borrowing would meet the 300 percent asset coverage requirement. Leverage augments returns on the upside and the downside, so it is associated with higher risk. And, as noted previously, one of the most important developments in the modern theory of finance is that risk is closely associated with the volatility (or standard deviation) of price movements over time. In short, this means that the higher the volatility, the higher is the risk.

Mutual Funds Become the Largest Intermediary in Financial Markets

Mutual funds continued to enjoy, on the other hand, a tremendous growth in assets under management, fueled by both net inflows of new money and, to a lesser

FIGURE 1-4   U.S. mutual funds: assets and numbers (dollar amounts in billions, year-end)

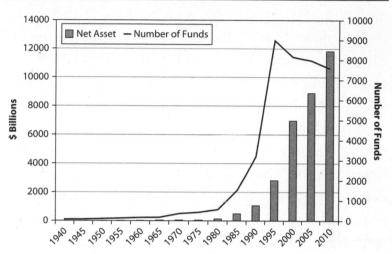

Source: Investment Company Institute Fact Book: 2012.

extent, rising asset prices. The mutual fund industry's data, shown in Figure 1-4, indicate that total net assets increased nearly eightfold from $134.8 billion on December 31, 1980, to $1,065.2 billion on December 31, 1990. Figure 1-2 shows that U.S. stock prices rose strongly, on average, over the 1980s, a period that also witnessed the first decade of a more than 30-year bull-market span in interest rates. Interestingly, the number of shareholder accounts rose less than fivefold over the same 10-year span, suggesting that institutional investors were increasingly using mutual funds to get access to U.S. stock prices and other assets. The growth in assets was accompanied by an expansion in the number of mutual funds, although this was only at about a sixfold pace. The complexity of asset-management strategies also continued to increase. The assets of money-market funds exploded in the late 1970s, and by December 31, 1980, the assets under management of these substitutes for cash and near-cash balances was at $76.4 billion, an amount larger than the net assets of equity mutual funds at $44.4 billion.

While the total net assets of both long-term equity and money-market mutual funds continued to grow rapidly in the 1980s, the real star of this era was bond funds. As noted previously, U.S. interest rates peaked at record levels in the early 1980s, and then longer-term U.S. interest rates began a more than 30-year bull market. The decline in interest rates fueled the returns for intermediate- and longer-term bond funds that spanned the investment styles from default-free U.S. government obligations to high-yield "junk" bonds. The total net assets of bond and hybrid mutual funds (funds that invest in a combination of equities and bonds) grew more than 23-fold over the 10-year period that ended December 31, 1990.

Investors Start Focusing on Hedge Funds

Because hedge funds were not required to register with the SEC or any other federal agency over this period, no one knows with certainty either the number of hedge funds or their assets under management in the 1980s. However, the strong investment performance of both equity- and fixed-income-oriented hedge funds became a much-discussed topic among wealthy individuals and representatives of foundations and endowments in the late 1980s and early 1990s. SEC rules prevented the investment managers of these vehicles from publicizing their results and advertisements were strictly prohibited, but word spread, nevertheless, about their investment results. Thus more and more assets found their way into the asset-management vehicles of hedge fund managers.

Although hedge funds are prohibited from using general advertising, U.S. security laws do not prevent private data providers from assembling and vending information about nonregistered investment vehicles. Two early proponents of this business were the Hennessey Group, which began recording data on hedge funds in 1987, and Hedge Fund Research (HFR), which started in 1992. HFR soon established itself as a premier source of data on the hedge fund industry, and it backfilled its database so that relatively complete information was available from January 1990 onward. Besides offering a database of information on individual hedge funds, HFR also became an index provider. This means that it grouped all of its reporting hedge funds into various categories that operate with similar investment styles or strategies and created peer-group indexes.

The HFR database indicates that 530 hedge funds existed on December 31, 1990, and these vehicles had total net assets of $38.9 billion. This pales somewhat compared with the total net assets of mutual funds. These vehicles had total net assets of $1,065.2 billion on the same date and reflected 3,079 mutual funds. Thus, at the beginning of the final decade of the twentieth century, the total net assets of mutual funds were 27 times larger than those of hedge funds, although the number of mutual funds was only about six times larger than hedge funds.

Both mutual funds and hedge funds continued to grow rapidly over the next 10 years (Figure 1-5). The mutual fund industry enjoyed bull markets in

FIGURE 1-5   Total net assets and number of mutual funds and hedge funds (dollar amounts in billions)

Year End	Mutual Funds		Hedge Funds	
	Total Net Assets	Number	Total Net Assets	Number
1990	$1,065	3,079	$39	530
1991	$1,393	3,403	$58	694
1992	$1,643	3,824	$96	937
1993	$2,070	4,534	$168	1,277
1994	$2,155	5,325	$167	1,654
1995	$2,811	5,725	$186	2,006
1996	$3,526	6,248	$257	2,392
1997	$4,468	6,684	$368	2,564
1998	$5,525	7,314	$375	2,848
1999	$6,846	7,791	$456	3,102
2000	$6,965	8,155	$491	3,335
2001	$6,975	8,305	$539	3,904
2002	$6,384	8,243	$626	4,598
2003	$7,204	8,125	$820	5,065
2004	$8,095	8,040	$913	5,782
2005	$8,891	7,974	$1,105	6,665
2006	$10,398	8,118	$1,465	7,241
2007	$12,002	8,026	$1,868	7,634
2008	$9,604	8,022	$1,407	6,845
2009	$11,113	7,663	$1,600	6,883
2010	$11,832	7,555	$1,917	7,200
2011	$11,627	7,555	$2,008	7,574
2012	$13,045	7,596	$2,252	7,940

Sources: Mutual funds: Investment Institute Fact Book: 2012; Hedge funds: Hedge Fund Research.

both equities and fixed-income instruments, and the number of U.S. households owning mutual fund shares soared to 47 million in 2000 versus less than 10 million in 1980. The types of mutual funds broadened further, and new and creative ways to market the investment vehicles helped to spur the growth. A new entrant to the investment-company space occurred in 1993 when the first exchange-traded '40 Act investment company, or *exchange-traded fund* (ETF), began operating. The first ETF was created when the SEC granted exemptive relief from the Investment Company Act of 1940 that would otherwise not allow the ETF structure. Indeed, the SEC's exemptive relief was limited to ETFs that track the performance of designated indexes until 2008. Figure 1-6 shows the total net assets and number of ETFs on an annual basis from 1993 through 2012. The figure also displays the total net assets of open-ended investment companies for the same period. Comparing the two series illustrates that the number and assets of ETFs grew slowly for the first two years or so but then accelerated quickly. The total net assets grew to more than 10 percent of total open-end investment-company assets by December 31, 2012.

Although always displaying volatility, the average annual return on the S&P 500 was about 18 percent for the 10-year period ending in 2000, and default-free 10-year U.S. Treasury note yields declined from 8.08 to 6.45 percent over the same span. As impressive as the growth in mutual funds was over the 1990s, the number

FIGURE 1-6   Total net assets and number of open-end mutual funds and ETFs (dollar amounts in billions). Totals exclude closed-end funds, unit investment trusts, and funds of funds

	Total Net Assets			Number of Vehicles		
		Mutual			Mutual	
Year-end	Total	Funds	ETFs	Total	Funds	ETFs
1993	$2,078.1	$2,070.0	$0.1	4,535	4,534	1
1994	$2,155.4	$2,155.3	$0.1	5,326	5,325	1
1995	$2,812.4	$2,811.3	$1.1	5,727	5,725	2
1996	$3,528.2	$3,525.8	$2.4	6,267	6,248	19
1997	$4,474.9	$4,468.2	$6.7	6,703	6,684	19
1998	$5,540.8	$5,525.2	$15.6	7,343	7,314	29
1999	$6,880.2	$6,846.3	$33.9	7,821	7,791	30
2000	$7,030.2	$6,964.6	$65.6	8,235	8,155	80
2001	$7,057.9	$6,974.9	$83.0	8,407	8,305	102
2002	$6,485.6	$6,383.5	$102.1	8,356	8,243	113
2003	$7,553.4	$7,402.4	$151.0	8,244	8,125	119
2004	$8,322.6	$8,095.1	$227.5	8,193	8,040	153
2005	$9,191.9	$8,891.1	$300.8	8,183	7,974	209
2006	$10,820.5	$10,397.9	$422.6	8,492	2,118	374
2007	$12,609.9	$12,001.5	$608.4	8,684	8,026	658
2008	$10,135.0	$9,603.7	$531.3	8,786	8,022	764
2009	$11,890.1	$11,113.0	$777.1	8,535	7,663	872
2010	$12,373.9	$11,381.9	$992.0	8,579	7,555	1,024
2011	$12,675.5	$11,627.4	$1,048.1	8,834	7,591	1,243
2012	$14,382.3	$13,045.2	$1,337.1	8,910	7,596	1,314

Source: Investment Company Institute Fact Book: 2013.

and assets under management of hedge funds virtually exploded over the same span. Figure 1-5 shows that the total net assets of hedge funds grew about 12.6 times over the decade and that the number of hedge funds grew about 6.3 times. Both rates of growth are about twice as fast as those for mutual funds.

The difficult financial market conditions since 2000 were initially a boon to the hedge fund industry. Hedge funds strongly outperformed mutual funds in the first few years of the new decade, and both the assets under management and the number of hedge funds grew much more rapidly than mutual funds. As market conditions became more difficult in the second half of the decade, and especially in 2008, both types of investment companies witnessed a decline in assets under management and a retracement of the number of vehicles in operation. The combination of sharply declining prices for equities, non-government-guaranteed fixed-income instruments, and real estate greatly affected the investment attitudes of both individual and institutional investors.

'40 Act Alternatives Solve a Need

One consequence of this turmoil was a much larger appetite for *risk-managed* financial assets. The myth of hedge funds being able to achieve "absolute returns" in all market conditions was discarded, but individual and even institutional investors wanted the risk controls of hedge funds plus the liquidity, transparency, and regulatory framework of mutual funds. This was an enormous boost to '40 Act alternative vehicles. Total net assets of the *hybrid* investment companies began to grow strongly, and the number of funds multiplied. Just as mutual funds had grown rapidly in the 1970s and 1980s and then the pace of hedge funds accelerated in the 1990s and early 2000s, '40 Act alternative investment funds are increasingly becoming the vehicle of choice for mass affluent, ultra-high-net-worth, and many institutional investors.

The growth of these liquid alternatives is coming from two distinct sources. A large proportion of existing mutual fund management companies are originating new strategies that produce the types of performance characteristics that most hedge funds deliver, and at the same time, these management companies are amending the investment objectives and characteristics of previously existing mutual funds to allow them to have many of the same features of hedge funds. In addition, a large number of hedge fund managers have realized that their hedge fund strategies can be effectively executed as '40 Act mutual funds with relatively few fundamental changes to the hedge fund strategies so that these investment managers are registering and operating new mutual fund vehicles.

It is, of course, too early to tell whether '40 Act mutual funds will exhibit the same type of growth as mutual funds in the 1970–1990 period and hedge funds in the 1990–2007 era. It seems reasonable to expect, however, that the growth will be strong because the investment proclivities of investors have experienced the sea change associated with the "great recession."[9]

2

The Strengths and Weaknesses
of Liquid Alternatives

As discussed in Chapter 1, Investment Company Act of 1940 ('40 Act) alternative vehicles, or liquid alternatives, are a hybrid vehicle that grew out of the growth and development of, initially, the mutual fund industry and, eventually, the hedge fund industry. Chapter 1 also indicated that the growth and market impact of hedge funds were relatively small in the early 1990s, but they accelerated over the 1997–2003 period. Very few market participants really understood hedge funds in their early years, and there was a need to educate the investing public.

What is a Hedge Fund?

The U.S. Securities and Exchange Commission (SEC) published, for example, a staff report on the growing hedge fund phenomenon in September 2003.[1] One of the more important questions that the SEC staff tried to answer was, "What is a hedge fund?" They were unable to concisely answer the question. Instead, the report stated that it is a term that "generally is used to refer to an entity that holds a pool of securities and perhaps other assets, whose interests are not sold in a registered public offering and which is not registered as an investment company under the Investment Company Act." The report added that in addition to trading equities, hedge funds may trade fixed-income securities, convertible securities, currencies, exchange-traded futures, over-the-counter derivatives, futures contracts, commodity options, and other nonsecurities investments. Furthermore, hedge funds may or may not use the hedging and arbitrage strategies that hedge funds historically employed, and many engage in relatively traditional long-only equity strategies. The staff classified hedge funds into three broad substrategies, and each had further substrategies of two or three categories.

The SEC staff undoubtedly leaned heavily on the categorization that Hedge Fund Research (HFR) had developed to assemble its hedge fund database and construct its peer-group indexes that are published, with a two-week lag, on a monthly basis. HFR publishes an industry-wide peer-group index, called the *HFRI Fund Weighted Composite Index*, as well as a large number of substrategy indexes. HFR has established, for example, four broad substrategy classifications (equity hedge, macro, event driven, and relative value), and each of these has a large number of further substrategies.

FIGURE 2-1   Hedge fund substrategies

Equity Hedge	Macro	Event Driven	Relative Value
Equity Market Neutral	Active Trading	Activist	Fixed Income-Asset Backed
Fundamental Growth	Commodity	Credit Arbitrage	Fixed Income-Conv. Arb.
Fundamental Value	Currency-Discretionary	Distressed/Restructuring	Fixed Income-Corporate
Quantitative Directional	Currency-Systematic	Merger Arbitrage	Fixed Income-Sovereign
Short Bias	Discretionary Thematic	Multi-Strategy	Multi-Strategy
Sector Funds	Multi-Strategy	Private Issues/Reg. D	Volatility
Multi-Strategy	Systematic Diversified	Special Situations	Yield Alternatives

Source: Hedge Fund Research.

Equity hedge is comprised, for example, of (1) equity market neutral, (2) fundamental growth, (3) fundamental value, (4) quantitative directional, (5) short bias, (6) sector funds, and (7) multistrategy. All the hedge funds that comprise these seven substrategies use an equity approach, mostly long/short, as their investment strategy. Figure 2-1 presents the substrategies for each of the four major substrategies. HFR publishes, on a monthly basis, a peer-group index for each of the substrategies as well as other hedge fund indexes.

Just as the total assets under management and number of hedge funds have grown over the last two decades, the asset composition of the hedge fund industry has shifted as well. Figure 2-2 shows the number of hedge funds and their total assets for each of the broad HFR substrategies at five-year intervals from 1990 through 2010. These data show that the macro

FIGURE 2-2   Number of Hedge Funds and assets under management (AUM) by major substrategy (dollar amounts in billions)

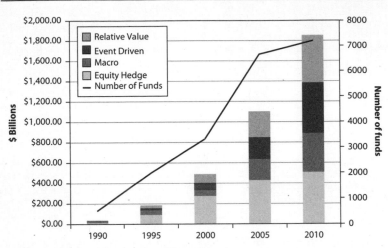

Source: Hedge Fund Research and Forward.

substrategy accounted for nearly two-fifths of the total hedge fund assets in 1990, but the proportion shrunk to less than one-fifth 20 years later. Figure 2-2 also shows that equity hedge was the industry's largest substrategy over the two decades, although it was 30 percent of overall hedge fund assets in 2010 versus 37 percent in 1990. Equity hedge funds grew to be more than half the total assets in 2000 because of rising stock prices and net inflows of new money, but the category failed to maintain the pace over the next 10 years. The lack of a meaningful gain in U.S. stock prices since 2000 and the continuing bull market in interest rates caused event-driven and relative-value hedge funds to each gain a substantial market share.

Chapter 1 suggested that while mutual funds and hedge funds share many similarities, there are also important differences between the two types of investment vehicles. Before discussing the attributes of '40 Act alternative mutual funds, it's useful to explore the differences between the two types of investment funds that spawned liquid alternatives. This will be done by focusing first on *structural* differences (how they are organized), next on *marketing* differences (how they are sold to investors), and finally on *operational* differences (how the investment vehicles operate in the markets).

Structural Differences

In the United States, all open-end, closed-end, and unit investment trust investment companies operate under the authority of the Investment Company Act of 1940. As noted briefly in Chapter 1, hedge funds are organized as limited-liability partnerships in the United States and thus avoid registering under the '40 Act because of the exemption provisions accorded under Sections 3(c)(1) and 3(c)(7) of the act. With regard to the number of investors, as can be seen in Figure 2-3, mutual funds are allowed an unlimited number of shareholders. Investment limited partnerships are designed, on the other hand, for a small number of investors. As a result, Section 3(c)(1) of the Act limits the number of investors (commonly referred to as *slots*) to 99, whereas Section 3(c)(7) vehicles are limited to 499 investors.

FIGURE 2-3   Structural differences between mutual funds and hedge funds

Type	Mutual Funds	Hedge Funds
Regulatory Mandate	Investment Company Act of 1940	Securities Act of 1933
Number of Investors	Unlimited	3(c)(1): 99 or less 3(c)(7): 499 or less
Ownership Structure	Mutual Fund	Private
Investor Qualifications	None	Accredited Investors: 3(c)(1) Qualified Purchasers: 3(c)(7)
Custody of Assets	Commercial Bank (Custodian)	Brokerage Firm (Prime Broker)
Taxation	Pass through to investors	Pass through to investors
U.S. IRS Reporting	1099	K-1
Governance	Board of Directors/Trustees	None

The '40 Act requires that investor assets be held in custody by a third-party bank, whereas no such restriction is in place on hedge funds. A general partner of a hedge fund will typically hold the fund's securities at a prime broker (usually a major financial intermediary that offers a variety of services), and the prime broker will, in turn, lend money and securities to support the hedge fund's leverage and short selling. Because the prime broker has custody of the assets, it has the ability to sell them in the market if concerns arise over the ability of the hedge fund to meet its obligations. Many hedge funds have been started, it should be noted, by individuals employed by these major financial intermediaries who show their trading prowess as a *proprietary trader* (or *prop trader*) for the institution.

A fund's governance structure is also markedly different for mutual funds and hedge funds. A mutual fund must have a board of directors/trustees who are charged with looking out for the best interests of the shareholders. These boards must hold regular meetings and are required to evaluate the quality of the investment advisor for the mutual fund and review the expenses being passed on to shareholders. In the case of a hedge fund, the hedge fund manager usually is the general partner, and the partnership is structured as a limited-liability entity. Investors are limited partners, so their liability is constrained to the amount that each limited partner has invested.

In the area of federal taxation, both mutual funds and hedge funds are pass-through vehicles that allow the tax burden to flow through to investors. Mutual funds issue Form 1099s annually to shareholders, whereas hedge funds issue Form K-1s to limited partners.

The Relationship between Long-Only Investing and Benchmarks

As mutual funds became more widely held by investors, many individuals looked for ways to evaluate mutual fund holdings: (1) Did they hold a mutual fund with an investment objective that was aligned with their expectations? (2) Was the mutual fund's portfolio manager performing well relative to his or her peers? (3) If the investor held more than one mutual fund, did the portfolio of mutual funds appear to benefit the investor? And so forth. Portfolio managers also wanted measures that would allow their portfolio-management capabilities to be evaluated objectively.

The first objective in portfolio performance measurement is to determine what it is being measured against. In the case of mutual funds, they are, by statute, required to be a diversified portfolios, so it is natural that either other mutual funds with similar investment objectives or stock-price indexes that are comprised of the types of securities that the mutual fund might hold are good candidates for a benchmark.

Stock-price indexes are, of course, almost as old as the stock exchanges themselves. The most famous stock-price index is probably the Dow Jones Industrial Average (DJIA). This index was created by Charles H. Dow, who cofounded the *Wall Street Journal* and Dow Jones & Company. The DJIA was first published on May 26, 1896. It was actually the second stock index created by Dow, because he also created the Dow Jones Transportation Index. The DJIA is a price-weighted index of 30 large, well-capitalized U.S. corporations, and the specific component companies change every few years. When the DJIA was first published, it was calculated by adding up the prices of the individual companies and dividing this sum by the number of issuers. However, every time a constituent company paid a cash or stock dividend, the DJIA's divisor is adjusted.

Although the DJIA remains a popular measure of the U.S. stock market, most market practitioners prefer capitalization-weighted indexes such as Standard & Poor's 500 Index (S&P 500). As the name implies, the S&P 500 is comprised of the stock prices of 500 large (mostly U.S.) corporations, and each company's total market value is calculated by multiplying the number of outstanding shares by the daily closing stock price. This value is summed and divided by 500 to arrive at the index's value.

If a mutual fund's investment objective is to pick the "best" large-capitalization U.S. companies, then the S&P 500 is probably a good benchmark for investors and the portfolio manager. If the manager is skilled at identifying over- and undervalued companies, then his or her performance results over time should be better than the return achieved by the index. Stock-price indexes can, of course, be created on any group of stock prices with similar characteristics. Accordingly, a mutual fund that restricts its holdings to, say, companies operating in the energy-extraction business can create an index of all, or most, of the energy-extraction stocks to serve as a benchmark for the mutual fund's portfolio.

Marketing Differences

Hedge funds are private placements, and they cannot be offered to the public at large. In fact, the investors must be knowledgeable and sophisticated. These terms are, of course, quite unspecific, and congressional legislators elected to fulfill this part of the statute, as can be seen in Figure 2-4, by requiring a *wealth test* for each limited-partnership investor. Each investor in a Section 3(c)(1) hedge fund must be accredited, and *accredited* is defined in Regulation D of the Securities Act of 1933. An *accredited* individual investor must have at least $1.0 million of liquid net worth or an annual income of at least $200,000 for the past two years (or joint income with their spouse above $300,000) and the reasonable expectation of reaching the same income level in the year of investment. An institutional investor must have at least $5.0 million of assets. There are, as well, separate provisions for family-owned companies and trustees.

FIGURE 2-4   Marketing differences between mutual funds and hedge funds

Type	Mutual Funds	Hedge Funds
Marketing	SEC/FINRA Rules	Limited to private placement requirements in security laws
Shareholder/Limited Partner Wealth Requirement	No Restrictions	3(c)(1): Accredited investors 3(c)(7): Qualified purchasers
Sales Documents	New shareholder must receive a prospectus	Limited partners rely on private placement memorandum and subscription documents
Customer Solicitation	Must meet SEC/FINRA rules	No public solicitation allowed and SEC/FINRA rules

In the case of a Section 3(c)(7) vehicle, where the limited-liability partnership can accept up to 499 investors, each investor must be a qualified purchaser. A *qualified purchaser* has a higher wealth standard: each individual must have at least $5 million of investable assets, and an "institutional" investor must have at least $25 million of investable assets.

The restriction on the number of investors, or slots, is the principal reason that hedge funds are considered vehicles for high-net-worth investors. If you are a hedge fund general partner and are offering a Section 3(c)(1) vehicle to investors, requiring a minimum investment of $100,000 per slot would limit the hedge fund's total *assets under management* (AUM) to only $9.9 million. In a similar fashion, the total AUM of a Section 3(c)(7) vehicle would be $49.9 million. As a result, most hedge funds have a minimum investment of $1 million, and many have even higher limits of $5 or $10 million. This results in the target audience of individual investors being, for the most part, ultra-high-net-worth (UHNW) investors, family offices, foundations, and endowments.

The '40 Act established all sales of mutual funds to be *new issues*, as defined in the Securities Act of 1933 ('33 Act), and investors must be provided with disclosure by means of prospectuses. The '33 Act also designated the SEC as the principal federal regulator for investment companies. In addition to the SEC, the securities industry established *self-regulatory organizations* (SROs) as entities that allow the industry to regulate itself. Initially called the *National Association of Security Dealers* (NASD), it formerly ran the NASDAQ stock exchange and NASD Regulation, Inc., which was one of Wall Street's self-regulating agencies. The NASDAQ became a public corporation in 2005, and the NASD sold its ownership share in 2006. In July 2007, the NASD merged its regulatory functions with the enforcement arm of the New York Stock Exchange (NYSE) to form the Financial Industry Regulatory Authority (FINRA). All mutual fund sales literature must meet the strict guidelines of SEC/FINRA regulatory requirements.[2]

In the case of hedge funds, limited partners (LPs) rely, first and foremost, on the private-placement memorandum prepared by the general partner (GP) for information about the partnership. The document stipulates the details of the investment structure. These documents are typically stamped "confidential" and numbered so that the GP knows who has a copy of the document. Doing so allows the GP to stay in compliance with federal and state solicitation rules. In addition, a *limited-partnership agreement* details the contract with the hedge fund and specifies the rights and obligations of the GP and the LPs alike. Finally, all subscribers must fill out a *subscription agreement* when electing to participate in the partnership. The subscription agreement requires the potential LP to attest to meeting the requirements for the type of hedge fund: Section 3(c)(1) or Section 3(c)(7). The subscription agreement also has the potential investor attesting that he or she, for individuals, and it, for institutions, fully understand the investment strategy and risks of the partnership.

Operational Differences

As noted earlier, all liquid alternative strategies must be registered with the SEC and adhere to the statutes and laws proscribed by the '40 Act and its various amendments. These operational differences are summarized in Figure 2-5. Chapter 1 also noted that hedge funds, from

FIGURE 2-5   Operational differences between mutual funds and hedge funds

Type	Mutual Funds	Hedge Funds
Investment Style	Mostly long only	Opportunistic/risk controlled focus
Investment Style	Returns relative to a benchmark	Absolute returns
Portfolio Pricing	Daily	Monthly
Fees	Management fee only	Management and performance fee
Leverage	Longs limited to 200% Shorts limited to 100%	No limitation other than discussed in private placement memorandum.
Bank borrowing	One-third of AUM	No limitation other than discussed in private placement memorandum.
Portfolion Concentration	IRS subchapter M requires at least 90% of a fund's gross income to be derived from dividends, interest, capital gains and payments from security loans. At the end of each quarter of fund's taxable year, at least 50% of the fund's total net assets must be cash, cash items, goverment securitites and investment in other securities. Any one issue can represent more than 5% of assets or more than 10% of voting securities of any one issuer.	No limits other than discussed in private placement memorandum.

their inception, embraced the concept of being both long and short securities in attempting to achieve their overall portfolio goals. This was, until fairly recently, in stark contrast to mutual funds, whose portfolio managers were overwhelmingly focused on holding long positions in their portfolios. This focus on long-only investing had a large impact on how mutual funds were organized, marketed, and evaluated.

Looking at the various substrategies listed in Figure 2-1 shows that many, but not all, of the strategies meet the various limitations on mutual funds. Certain hedge funds, however, operate in ways that disqualify them from offering the strategy as a '40 Act product. The most onerous of the '40 Act limitations is the *core requirement* that open-ended registered investment companies must be able to offer and redeem shares on a daily basis, and this requires the ability to price every security in the portfolio on a daily basis. Portfolio pricing on a daily basis sounds easy, and it is for most of the securities held by U.S. mutual funds. This reflects the fact that the overwhelming majority of their portfolio securities are continuously traded in two-way markets each and every trading day. Other, more esoteric securities do not trade regularly, however. In fact, some of them might go weeks without a transaction. The most prominent group of these types of securities that are used by hedge fund portfolio managers is distressed securities. *Distressed securities* are securities of companies or government entities that are in default, under bankruptcy protection,

or "in distress" and likely heading toward such a condi-
tion. The most common distressed securities are bonds
and bank debt.

Performance Fees and High-Water Marks

Assume, for example, that a hedge fund manager
has total net assets of $10.0 million over a one-year
period and one limited partner. For added simplicity, also assume that all investment gains or losses
occur on the final day of the year. If the management fee is 2 percent, then the manager will earn
$0.2 million from the management fee in year one.
Next, assume that the hedge fund gained 10 percent on the last day of the year. The performance
fee earns the manager an additional $0.2 million of
compensation, and the LP investor earns a gain of
8 percent rather than 10 percent. However, if in year
two the hedge fund drops by –10.1 percent, then
the manager again earns the management fee of
$0.2 million but no performance fee. Next, assume
that the hedge fund increases by 10 percent in year
three. Once again, the management fee is $0.2
million, but the performance fee is not paid because
the first 10 percent of the gain was already earned in
year one. This simplified example demonstrates that
the hedge fund manager maximizes his or her fee
income by avoiding losses. Moreover, hedge fund
investors are a fickle lot, and many will redeem from
a hedge fund if it does not earn consistently positive

returns (i.e., absolute returns). Finally, the remuneration of most hedge fund employees is highly dependent on the performance fees, so if a portfolio manager goes into a deep drawdown, it is likely that the hedge fund will have a problem with employee retention. Thus, for a variety of reasons, hedge fund portfolio managers/GPs are strongly motivated to manage their funds with a focus on absolute returns.

One of the four HFR hedge fund substrategies shown in Figure 2-1 is *event driven*. This means, broadly speaking, that the strategy attempts to take advantage of events such as mergers and restructurings that can result in the short-term mispricing of a company's securities. Two of the event-driven substrategies, distressed/restructuring and private issues/Reg. D, largely employ securities that are not priced or traded on a daily basis. These two categories, especially the distressed category, constitute a meaningful portion of hedge fund assets. In addition, a large portion of some of the other substrategies in the event-driven category, such as multistrategy and special situations, may use securities that are not priced regularly, so these types of strategies will also be eliminated from being used as '40 Act alternative fund investment strategies.[3]

It was noted earlier that mutual funds and other registered investment companies are limited in the degree of leverage a fund can employ in its investment

strategies. It also was stated that a very large proportion of hedge funds use leverage to generate, hopefully, attractive returns. Thus it is clear that '40 Act
alternative funds can, like all mutual funds, use leverage to enhance their returns, but they are, as a group,
constrained relative to hedge funds with the amount
of leverage they can employ. Returning to Figure 2-1,
there are a number of successful hedge fund strategies
that employ three times, four times, and even higher
amounts of leverage to generate acceptable returns
for their investors. In the relative-value substrategy,
for example, convertible-arbitrage, asset-backed, sov-
ereign, and yield alternatives vehicles may employ a
degree of leverage that disqualifies each of them from
being run as a '40 Act alternative fund.

In summary, this chapter has highlighted the major
similarities and dissimilarities between mutual funds and
hedge funds. Although both investment vehicles share
some of the same characteristics, their differences dictate
that they be organized, marketed, and operated in ways
that are often at odds with each other.

3

How Do '40 Act Alternative Mutual Funds Make Money for Their Investors

Most investors have only a vague idea, at best, about how an alternative investment portfolio manager earns returns on a portfolio of securities. Not surprisingly, there are, of course, a wide range of strategies available to these managers. This chapter discusses the major investment strategies employed by Investment Company Act of 1940 ('40 Act) alternative vehicles and explains how each broad category is managed for investors.

It's useful, however, to first broadly review how hedge fund portfolio managers attempt to earn positive excess returns, or *alpha*, in their activities. What exactly is alpha? *Alpha* is a concept that was developed in the early years of *modern portfolio theory* (MPT). A debate among academicians and other researchers surfaced in the late 1960s and 1970s about whether professional portfolio managers were earning returns for their investors that were commensurate with the risks that they were taking.

MPT postulated that a portfolio manager could earn a return that was below, at, or above the expected return for a portfolio if the *riskiness* of the portfolio could be estimated properly. It was suggested that returns could be high, but this may largely reflect the fact that the portfolio was allocated to very risky securities. It was possible, therefore, for the portfolio's return to be high but below where it should be given the riskiness of the portfolio holdings. Similarly, a portfolio's return could be below the return on a broadly based market index over time, but if the portfolio was comprised of relatively low-risk stocks, then the return could be in excess of its expected value. All this was predicated on the idea that portfolios could be judged against a market index adjusted for risk and the result evaluated as to whether the return, over time, was above or below its *expected value*.

Early proponents of MPT encapsulated this theory into the *capital asset pricing model* (CAPM). This model states that a portfolio's return can be evaluated by subtracting the risk-free rate (generally measured by, say, three-month U.S. Treasury bill rates) from the periodic return on the portfolio over time and comparing this return to the overall market return (generally measured by the Standard & Poor's 500 Index), also reduced by the risk-free rate, adjusted by the relative riskiness of the portfolio, or *beta*. If the portfolio manager has true *skill*, the portfolio's return will be greater than the risk-adjusted return on the market portfolio, and this difference is called *alpha*. Of course, there is no assurance that the portfolio's alpha will be positive. It could be zero or negative.

As was discussed earlier, the early studies suggested that the mutual fund industry's average alpha was somewhat negative, but these results were hotly debated by academicians and other researchers for years and years. In fact, the debate is still continuing. However, rather than focusing on each side's arguments, let's hold this off until Chapter 8. In the meantime, certain proponents of the hedge fund industry argue that hedge fund manager results are superior to mutual fund manager results because their investment style and tools allow these new vehicles to achieve returns that are well above their expected returns (i.e., positive alpha) adjusted for the riskiness (beta) of the hedge funds. Rather than focusing further on the two sides of this debate, this chapter investigates how portfolio managers running alternative investment strategies *attempt* to earn positive excess return, or alpha, for their investors. Let's begin by reviewing the four major types of hedge funds, as classified by Hedge Fund Research's (HFR's) broad substrategies.

Equity Hedge

As the name implies, these hedge funds are focused on the global equity market. Equity hedge portfolio managers typically maintain positions, both long and short, in equity and/or equity derivative securities. The managers employ a very wide range of techniques to identify both under- and overvalued securities. These include both quantitative and qualitative, or fundamental, techniques. Some managers focus on particular sectors, such as health sciences, or total-capitalization segments, such as companies with relatively small total capitalizations. The portfolio managers usually attempt to earn excess returns on both the securities selected for the long *book*, that is, undervalued equities, as well as equities sold short, where the manager thinks the securities are *overvalued*. Most equity hedge portfolio managers typically maintain a *long bias* in their holdings, although a small subset of managers is *short biased*. Most long-biased managers hold anywhere from 50 to 150 percent of their equity capital in long positions, and these manager typically hold 25 to 100 percent of their equity capital in short positions. Adding an equity hedge fund's long positions (plus cash) to its short positions, each expressed as a percentage of the manager's total capital, is a manager's *gross exposure*. Subtracting the short exposure from the long exposure, both as percentages of capital, is an equity hedge fund's *net exposure*. Figure 2-1 shows that HFR further subdivides equity hedge into seven substrategies.

Understanding Performance Fees

Most mutual fund portfolio managers employ a *long-only* approach to achieving their investment objectives, whereas it is very common for hedge fund managers to use a mix of both *longs* and *shorts*. Risk management is a key objective of these portfolio managers because almost all hedge funds have a remuneration schedule that has a management fee (typically 2 percent annually of total net assets) plus a performance fee of 20 percent of annual gains. Performance fees also have *high-water marks* that limit the payment of the performance fee to only being paid once.

Macro

Investment managers who focus on a broad range of strategies and depend on movements in macroeconomic variables are grouped into the macro category. Many of these managers trade in the global equity, fixed-income, currency, and commodity markets. A large number of these managers trade systematic strategies that rely on momentum and other factors, although many of these portfolio managers focus on fundamental factors or some combination of systematic and fundamental factors. Holding periods for individual positions vary widely in the macro category, with some managers trading daily and intraday, whereas others may hold positions for weeks or months. Figure 2-1 shows the seven broad substrategies that are classified as macro by HFR.

Event Driven

Event-driven hedge funds are vehicles where portfolio managers take positions in companies that are currently, or prospectively, involved in some sort of corporate transaction. These events include transactions such as mergers or restructurings, tender offers, shareholder buybacks, debt exchanges, security issuance, or other capital-structure adjustments. The strategy also incorporates companies undergoing financial distress. These managers may engage in transactions that use different securities of a company's capital structure (widely referred to as *capital-structure arbitrage*). Most of these transactions are predicated on company-specific developments, although it is not known with certainty when or if the transaction or transactions are going to take place. Figure 2-1 shows the seven substrategies that HFR classifies as event-driven.

Relative Value

Hedge funds that hold positions that rely on the realization of an ex ante valuation discrepancy are called *relative-value vehicles*. Relative value is primarily an *arbitrage* investment strategy that seeks to take advantage of price differentials between related financial instruments by simultaneously buying and selling the different securities. If the a priori security relationship is realized, a profit likely will accrue to the investment vehicle that has established the positions. Many relative-value strategies are highly quantitative in their underlying investment thesis, and portfolio managers may rely on leverage, in certain cases, relatively large leverage or gearing, for the positions to be acceptably profitable. Managers employ a variety of fundamental and quantitative techniques to establish investment theses, and security types range broadly across equity, fixed-income, derivative, and other security classes. Unlike event-driven strategies, relative-value hedge funds do not typically rely on a corporate transaction outcome for success. Figure 2-1 showed the seven substrategies that HFR classifies as relative value.

'40 Act Alternative Sub Strategies

In a manner similar to HFR, different vendors of mutual fund data have created strategy categorization schemes for '40 Act alternative vehicles. Morningstar and Strategic Insights have each categorized, for example, the vehicles into seven substrategies: equity long/short, bear market, currency, market neutral, multialternative, nontraditional bond, and managed futures. It's useful to examine each of these strategies to ascertain how an investor can benefit from allocating capital to them.

Chapter 1 stated that only four '40 Act alternative vehicles were operating as of December 31, 1985, and these had combined total net assets of only $122.0 million. All four of the vehicles are still operating, although almost all of them have had meaningful changes over their existence, and they also have had varying degrees of success.[1] The earliest of these funds began operation on December 7, 1977, and it is called the *Gateway Fund*. The Gateway Fund was and still is a fund with a strategy that invests in a broadly diversified portfolio of U.S.

common stocks while attempting to hedge some or all of the fund's equity-market risk exposure. This means that the fund's portfolio managers attempt to lower the fund's volatility and risk of loss from holding common stocks. The portfolio managers sell stock index calls to generate income and simultaneously buy stock index puts to protect the value of the portfolio if the overall stock market suffers a decline. This may not sound too revolutionary in today's market, but the Securities and Exchange Commission (SEC) only authorized the Chicago Board Options Exchange (CBOE) to initiate trading in standardized exchange-traded stock options on April 26, 1973 (initially call options only). The CBOE moved into its own building the following year, and the SEC eventually authorized put options in early 1977.

The total net assets of the Gateway Fund have grown relatively steadily since 1985 and, on December 31, 2012, reached an impressive $7.0 billion. The management company for the fund, Gateway Investment Advisors, was acquired, it should be noted, by Natixis Global Asset Management in 2008 and is one of several investment groups run by the now-parent company. The Gateway Fund's fact sheet states that the fund's "strategy" was changed at the beginning of 1988 and that, since that time, the fund has earned an average annual rate of return of 7.38 percent. This is below the rate of return on the Standard & Poor's 500 Index (S&P 500) over the same period of 10.04 percent. However, the fund's investment objective aims at "capturing the majority of returns associated with equity market investments while exposing investors to less risk than other equity investments." The same fact sheet points out that the volatility of the fund was only 6.88 percent over the period, whereas the volatility of the S&P 500 was 15.99 percent over the same span. Therefore, the fund's return was about three-fourths of the index's return, but the volatility of the fund was less than half the volatility of the index.

Using Return and Volatility to Assess Performance

Prior to the widespread adoption of computers and machine-accessible databases in the middle to late 1960s, mutual funds were evaluated solely on their rates of return over, say, several annual periods. A mainstay for mutual fund investors was the industry's statistical "bible," Arthur Wiesenberger's *Investment Companies and Their Securities*. The book was updated annually, and each mutual fund with at least a 10-year track record would have a full page devoted to it. The key statistic/exhibit was a 10-year *mountain chart* that showed how much a $10,000 investment (less the initial sales charge) grew to over the 10-year period. Because each annual addition ended on December 31, the individual mutual fund results were readily comparable with one another.

(continued)

The early years of computers allowed these time series of investment returns to be analyzed with techniques that were heretofore statistically possible but realistically too difficult and time-consuming. Early advances in economics and finance in this era postulated that risk could be measured statistically by a proxy: the variability of the return series over time. Early pioneers included Harry Markowitz and William Sharpe, both of whom won the Nobel Prize in economics for their contributions. The early work launched an avalanche of advancements in finance, and rates of return and their standard deviations became a common measure of investment performance.

A few months later, on July 3, 1978, the second '40 Act alternative was offered to the investing public: the *Touchtone Dynamic Equity Fund* (originally called the *Old Mutual Analytic Fund*). It, too, was a strategy based on controlling equity-market risk/volatility by using both call and put options in an attempt to dampen swings while achieving an acceptable return for investors. Using the fund's Y class of shares, the fund has achieved an average annual rate of return of 8.54 percent since its inception versus 11.58 percent for the S&P 500. The fund's total net assets have not fared too well, however, since they stood at only $20.0 million at the end of 2012.

Assessing the Current Size of the '40 Act Alternatives Universe

It was pointed out in Chapter 2 that the SEC was unable to precisely define what was and was not a hedge fund in it staff report published in 2003. Similarly, it is a daunting task to estimate both the number and total net assets of '40 Act alternatives because no one has produced a clear definition of what constitutes a liquid alternative strategy.

To assert some order in this chaos, this book relies on the earliest efforts of Morningstar to define the types of mutual funds that can logically be classified as '40 Act alternatives. Morningstar initially grouped the funds into seven substrategies: (1) equity long/short, (2) nontraditional bond, (3) bear market, (4) market neutral, (5) currency, (6) multialternative, and (7) managed futures. As Figure 3-1 shows, these seven categories constituted, as of December 31, 2012, a total of 368 investment vehicles with total net assets of $165.5 billion. However, Morningstar Direct lists an additional 14 substrategies that it considers "nonmainstream" investment objectives, and these include three trading-inverse categories (commodities, debt, and equity), three trading-leveraged categories (commodities, debt, and equity), one trading-miscellaneous category, five commodity categories (agriculture, broad basket, energy, industrial metal, miscellaneous), and one volatility category. When these vehicles

FIGURE 3-1   '40 Act alternative funds by substrategy (billions of dollars)

Year-end	Equity Long/Short		Nontraditional Bond		Bear Market		Market Neutral		Currency		Multi-Alternative		Managed Futures	
	No.	TNA	No.	TNA	No.	TNA	No.	TNA	No.	TNA	No.	TNA	No.	TNA
1985	2	$0.10	1	n.m.	1	n.m.	–	–	–	–	–	–	–	–
1990	2	$0.10	1	n.m.	1	$0.70	2	n.m.	2	$0.10	–	–	–	–
1995	3	$0.30	1	$0.20	3	$0.50	3	$0.30	2	$0.40	–	–	–	–
2000	7	$1.90	3	$0.10	11	$0.70	7	$1.20	3	$0.10	–	–	–	–
2005	18	$7.50	7	$3.80	21	$2.80	10	$6.30	9	$1.90	5	$2.00	–	–
2010	55	$19.30	28	$48.70	27	$4.50	24	$17.40	23	$9.20	42	$10.50	11	$4.40
2012	92	$28.50	50	$67.90	29	$7.00	45	$19.70	28	$13.00	76	$20.10	48	$9.20

No., Number of Funds; TNA, Total Net Assets

Source: Hedge Fund Research and Forward.

and their total net assets are added to the previous Morningstar data, the total number of vehicles on December 31, 2012, jumps to 846, and the net assets total up to $375.4 billion.

Other mutual fund data vendors also have categorized '40 Act alternatives, and their substrategy categories are similar but not identical to those of Morningstar. Strategic Insight, for example, lists 31 substrategies. Alternative-U.S. equity accounts for 12 of these, alternative-international U.S. equity totals 5, and alternative-bond amounts to 3 substrategies. In addition, Strategic Insight has nine commodity subcategories, one currency category, and one global asset-allocation group. Many of Strategic Insight's subcategories are similar to Morningstar's, but many are not. Totaling up the number of investment companies identified by the Strategic Insight substrategies results in 1,148, and these funds have total net assets of $723.9 billion.

An attempt was made at Forward to reconcile the Morningstar and Strategic Insight databases of liquid alternatives. The two databases were merged, and the vehicles that appeared in both were identified and not double counted. This exercise produced a vehicle count of 1,244 mutual funds, and these funds had total net assets of $824.1 million on December 31, 2012.

The third liquid alternative fund that spans the entire 23-year period is the First Pacific Advisors (FPA) New Income Fund. The original fund was founded in 1969, but FPA took over the investment management in July 1984. The fund's fact sheet states that the FPA's inception was July 11, 1984, and performance data are available from July 1, 1984, onward. According to this document, the fund has earned an average annual rate of return of 7.97 percent since inception. The fund's investment objective is current income and long-term total return, with capital preservation also a consideration. FPA New Income Fund also seeks to generate a positive absolute return. The investment manager attempts to achieve this through a combination of income and capital appreciation, and it employs a total-return strategy using investments in fixed-income securities that focus on income, appreciation, and capital preservation. Market opportunity dictates emphasis across each of these three areas. The fund's total net assets were $5.0 billion on December 31, 2012.

The last of the four original '40 Act alternative vehicles that is still in operation is the Gabelli Comstock Capital Value Fund, an investment vehicle formed on October 10, 1985. The portfolio managers are currently Charles L. Minter and Martin Weiner. Charles Minter was one of the founders of Comstock Partners, Inc., an investment-management company formed in 1986, and Martin Weiner has been co-portfolio manager since 1999. Mario Gabelli's GAMCO Investors, Inc., is the investment adviser because the original investment advisor (Comstock Partners) was acquired by GAMCO in 2000.

The Comstock Capital Value Fund seeks to maximize total return, consisting of capital appreciation and current income. The fund can use a variety of investment strategies, including puts, options, and short sales, together with its investments in fixed-income securities. The fund's total net assets on December 31, 2012, were $70.0 million, and an inspection of its holdings shows that the great majority of its equity positions were short positions, and the portfolio managers use the proceeds of these trades to invest in a pool of fixed-income securities. The fund's average annual rate of return since inception is –3.08 percent versus an average annual rate of return of 10.71 percent for the S&P 500 over the same period. Clearly, this is not a fund for every investor. However, a short-biased fund may have attractive features for an investor seeking to manage the risk of a portfolio.

Just as the four original '40 Act alternative mutual funds have had varying degrees of success in the marketplace, the head and tail winds of financial markets have had an impact on the growth of the various substrategies of the funds. Figure 3-1 shows that only four more liquid alternative funds were offered to investors over the next five years. Two of these were currency funds, and two were market-neutral funds.

The first currency fund was the Lord Abbet Emerging Markets Currency Fund. The fund's inception was September 30, 1988, and its investment objective is long-term growth of capital and current income through investing in currencies of emerging markets. The portfolio manager seeks to identify currencies of countries where the positive fundamentals are not fully reflected in the currency's relative value. It's worth noting that in pursuing its investment objective, the fund may invest substantially in forward foreign-currency contracts, which are a type of derivative instrument, and the fund also may invest in other types of derivatives, including options, futures contracts, and swap agreements. The fund has achieved a 5.61 percent average annual rate of return thus far in its lifetime, and the fund's total net assets on December 31, 2012, were $446.0 million.

The second currency fund, the Franklin/Templeton Hard Currency Fund, started about one year later, but its investment objective is to focus on the currencies that protect against depreciation of the U.S. dollar relative to other currencies by investing in money-market instruments denominated in currencies of countries whose economic policies have historically resulted in low rates of inflation. The fund has achieved a 4.37 percent annual return since inception, and its asset were $519.0 million on December 31, 2012.

The first market-neutral alternative mutual fund was started at the end of January 1989. Westchester Capital Management claims that the fund is market neutral because it typically invests at least 80 percent of its total assets in companies involved in publicly announced mergers, takeovers, and other corporate reorganizations. Two principal types of mergers are possible: a cash merger and a stock merger. In a *cash merger*, an acquirer proposes to purchase the shares of the target for a certain price in cash. Until the acquisition is completed, the stock of the target typically trades below the purchase price. An arbitrageur buys the stock of the target and makes a gain if the acquirer ultimately buys the stock. For most of its merger arbitrage investments, the fund's potential profit is equal to the difference between the price at which it acquires the target company's shares and their expected value on completion of the transaction. The fund did not attract many new investors in its early years, but it had over $1.0 billion of net assets at the end of 2000, and it grew to $4.42 billion as of December 31, 2012.

The second market-neutral alternative mutual fund was the Calamos Market Neutral Income Fund. The fund uses, according to its fact sheet, two distinct strategies, convertible arbitrage and covered call writing, with the aim of maximizing current income and achieving a low correlation against the broad U.S. equity market. The fund's portfolio-management team employs an investment process that considers global macroeconomic factors and investment themes. The team conducts both fundamental and quantitative research to evaluate the source, sustainability, and risk of investment opportunities. The team manages a diversified portfolio, managing risk at the portfolio and individual-security levels.

Convertible arbitrage involves the simultaneous purchase of convertible securities and the short sale of the same issuer's common stock. The premise of the strategy is that the convertible is sometimes priced inefficiently relative to the underlying stock for reasons that range from illiquidity to market psychology. The number of shares sold short usually reflects a delta-neutral or market-neutral ratio. As a result, under normal market conditions, the fund's portfolio manager expects the combined position to be insensitive to small fluctuations in the price of the underlying stock. However, maintaining a market-neutral position may require rebalancing transactions, a process called *dynamic delta hedging*. The fund has earned a 4.98 percent average annual rate of return since its inception (September 4, 1990), its annualized standard deviation is only 5.01 percent, and its total net assets were $2,459.0 million on December 31, 2012.

The five-year period ending in December 1995 witnessed continued slow growth in '40 Act alternative mutual funds. Additional single vehicles were started in both the equity long/short and market-neutral substrategies, and two bear market funds began being offered to investors. The long/short fund was the Caldwell & Orkin Market Opportunity Fund. This fund's investment objective is a more typical equity long/short mandate: it seeks to outperform the S&P 500 over a full market cycle with less volatility.

The investment manager's webpage presents the team's process, and it's similar to those of other equity long/short managers, so reviewing it is instructive.[2] The manager states that it uses a "catalyst-driven, multidimensional, disciplined investment process focusing on active asset allocation, security selection, and surveillance" to achieve the fund's investment objective. *Active asset allocation* refers to the way the manager determines the balance of different types of assets in the fund at any given time. *Security selection* refers to the way the fund chooses the securities to buy or sell short. *Surveillance* refers to how the manager monitors the portfolio. Because the fund's process is explained in detail in its materials available to the public, I have paraphrased the discussion of longs, shorts, and fixed-income plus cash.[3]

1. *Long portfolio.* The long portfolio is comprised of securities that company research indicates may increase in price. This portion of the fund's portfolio consists primarily of common stock, exchange-traded funds (ETFs), and listed call options that the managers have purchased. When the portfolio team is positive on a particular company, it will buy the common stock of that company and/or listed call options that permit the fund to purchase that company's common stock at a fixed price for a limited time. When the manager is positive on overall stock markets, sectors of the stock market, or specific industries, the fund may buy ETFs that

track the performance of the appropriate markets, sectors, or industries. The fund also may buy listed call options that permit it to purchase the relevant ETF at a fixed price for a limited time.

How does the manager pick positions for the long portfolio? The manager selects individual long-stock positions by identifying companies that he or she believes are experiencing positive changes that may lead to a rise in their stock prices. Factors considered may include (1) acceleration of earnings and/or profits, (2) positive changes in management personnel or structure, (3) new product developments, and (4) positive changes in variables that indicate strengthening in a company's industry. If the manager is bullish on the overall market, he or she will try to increase the percentage of the fund's assets invested in the long portfolio relative to the size of the overall fund portfolio. If the manager believes that the outlook is positive and the stock market may rise, then he or she positions the portfolio to be long the market as a whole or long a particular market sector, and the fund may purchase one or more ETFs that track a stock market index or a particular sector of the market.

2. *Short portfolio.* The short portfolio is comprised of securities the investment manager's research team believes may decrease in price. This portion of the fund's portfolio consists

primarily of common stock and ETFs the investment manager has borrowed and sold short. The
short portfolio at times also may include listed
put options the fund has purchased. When the
manager is negative on a particular company
and research indicates that the company's stock
may decrease in price, the manager may sell short
the common stock of the company. If the price
of the stock sold short decreases before the position is closed, the fund will make money. If it
increases, the fund loses money. The fund also
may purchase listed put options that permit it
to sell that company's stock at a fixed price for
a limited time. When the manager is negative
on overall stock markets, sectors of the stock
market, or specific industries, the manager will
sell short ETFs that track the performance of
the appropriate markets, sectors, or industries.
The fund also may purchase listed put options
that permit it to sell the relevant ETF for a fixed
price for a limited time. A listed put option generally may increase in value when the underlying
security decreases in value. When the investment
manager uses short positions or put options, the
fund's portfolio is considered to be *hedged* so that
it is not fully exposed to the price movements
and volatility of the broader market in an effort
to reduce the fund's overall risk. The portfolio
manager sells securities short or purchase listed

put options to (1) manage or hedge exposure to perceived market risk, (2) preserve capital and potentially profit during a falling stock market, and (3) make money when the manager thinks a particular security's price will decline.

How does the manager pick positions for the short portfolio? The manager selects the individual short positions by identifying companies that he or she believes are experiencing negative changes that may cause their stock prices to fall. The manager evaluates factors similar to those evaluated for the long portfolio. These factors may include (1) deceleration of earnings or profits or acceleration of losses, (2) negative changes in management personnel or structure or failure to address management problems, (3) new product developments by a company's competitors, and/or (4) negative changes in variables that indicate weakening in a company's industry.

When the manager is bearish, he or she typically tries to increase the percentage of the assets invested in the short portfolio relative to the size of the overall fund portfolio. These can be attractive short candidates. In addition, if the manager believes that the outlook for the stock market is negative and may experience declines, then the manager will short the market as a whole or short a particular market sector rather than individual stocks. The manager also may purchase listed put options as a hedge against declines in individual stocks, sectors, or the stock market as a whole.

3. *Cash/money-market/fixed-income securities.* This portion of the fund's portfolio includes cash, cash equivalents (e.g., money-market funds and/or U.S. Treasury notes), and bonds (i.e., corporate or government bonds), although the manager generally emphasizes cash equivalents more than bonds. The corporate bonds purchased by the fund may have any maturity and be of any rating or quality as long as the investment manager believes that it is consistent with the fund's investment objective.

The next '40 Act alternative fund to join the roster in this period was the Gabelli ABC Fund. The Gabelli ABC Fund's stated investment objective is to achieve total returns that are attractive to investors in various market conditions without excessive risk of capital loss. The investment manager focuses the fund on arbitrage strategies, that is, investing in event-driven situations such as announced mergers, spin-offs, split-ups and liquidations, and reorganizations. If the portfolio manager does not perceive there to be a sufficient number of such arbitrage opportunities to employ all the firm's capital, then the fund may hold a significant portion of its assets in U.S. Treasury bills as it awaits opportunities. The fund also may invest in value-oriented common stocks and convertible securities.[4]

Bear-market funds are the next two liquid alternative vehicles that came to market. The second of these to come to market was the Federated Prudent Bear Fund, a vehicle that began on December 31, 1995. The fund's investment objective is capital appreciation, and it attempts to achieve it by seeking to help investors benefit from a declining U.S. stock market through the convenience of an actively managed bear fund. It focuses primarily on strategic short selling along with investments in stocks of companies that mine or explore for precious metals or other natural resources. It has achieved negative correlation historically with major U.S. and international asset classes.

Bear-Market Funds Proliferate

Figure 3-1 shows that the number of '40 Act alternatives offered to investors proliferated over the second half of the 1990s, with equity long/short and bear-market funds leading the charge. The number of equity long/short vehicles jumped from 3 at the end of 1995 to 7 at the end of 2000, and the number of bear-market funds increased by 8 to 11. The next-largest category showing an increase was market-neutral vehicles. In all, thirty-one '40 Act alternative mutual funds were operating by December 31, 2000. In terms of total net assets, the equity long/short category, at $1.9 billion, was the largest, followed by market neutral ($1.2 billion), bear market ($0.7 billion), and nontraditional bond ($0.1 billion).

U.S. equity prices posted overall strong gains over this period, although the Federal Reserve System had to step in and arrange the bailout and eventual liquidation of Long Term Capital Management (LTCM), a multistrategy hedge fund that specialized in arbitrage strategies that employed considerable leverage.[5]

The market disruption caused by the 1998 currency crises in Southeast Asia and the default of the ruble by the Russian Republic turned out to be rather short-lived events in global markets. U.S. stock prices rose sharply over most of the 1990s, and this culminated in what is now termed the *dot-com bubble*. Stock-price gains accelerated in 1999, when the S&P 500 rose 21.04 percent and the NASDAQ soared 85.59 percent. This bull market did not last much longer, however, because both indexes peaked in March 2000 and then posted sharp declines for the next two years. The sharp erosion in equity valuations cooled the desire of many market participants for equity-related vehicles, but interest rates continued their long decline over the period, and as a result, the demand for more income-oriented liquid alternative vehicles was boosted. Figure 3-1 shows that additional nontraditional bond, market-neutral, bear-market, and the first multialternative vehicles were offered to investors over the five-year period ending in December 2005.

Many of the bear-market funds that started in this period were *inverse-index products*, some of which were offered with "two times" exposures. In fact, of the

11 bear-market funds that were operating as of the end of December 2000, 8 were inverse-index products and only 3 were funds with portfolio managers that attempted to identify individual issues that are overvalued and then enter into short sales of the stocks. Inverse-index products have been controversial since they were first offered to investors. Many financial institutions take the view that short selling and the inherent risks are not well understood by most investors, so they have limited the access of many clients to inverse-index funds, especially those that offer two and three times exposures to the index.

The December 2000–December 2005 period witnessed an almost doubling of the number of '40 Act alternative vehicles to 70 and a fivefold increase in assets under management (AUM) to $24.3 billion. Figure 3-1 shows that most of the growth occurred in the equity long/short and market-neutral substrategies, but multialternative vehicles began to grow popular as well. Multialternative funds are, as the name implies, a group of strategies that, taken together, has attractive expected-return/risk characteristics. These types of vehicles can be largely divided into two classes: (1) a fund of funds where a manager selects a fund from other third-party managers and (2) a fund of funds where the investment manager selects a variety of funds from vehicles that his or her investment management company offers to investors. A combination of the two is also possible.

Managed Futures Enter the Fray

The most recent major substrategy to enter the liquid alternatives universe is *managed futures*. Managed futures funds will be discussed more fully in Chapter 6, but their brethren, *commodity trading advisors vehicles* (CTAs) have been available to investors for decades. Although many of these CTAs have relatively small initial-investment requirements, investors must declare themselves to be *accredited*. Moreover, most U.S.-registered financial advisors are registered with the SEC by successfully completing the Series 7 exam, administered by Financial Industry Regulatory Authority (FINRA), but CTAs can only be sold by financial advisors that successfully pass the National Futures Association's (NFA's) Series 3 exam, also administered by FINRA.[6] Despite these barriers, CTAs have been marketed to investors for more than 50 years, and a major CTA index provider, BarclayHedge, estimates that the amount of CTAs outstanding on December 31, 2012, was $329.6 billion.

Managed futures mutual funds were first offered to investors in 2007, and the concept spread quickly. Figure 3-1 shows that 11 managed futures funds were in existence by December 31, 2010, and these funds had total net assets of $4.4 billion. The number of vehicles rose to 48 as of December 31, 2012, and the AUM climbed to $9.2 billion.

4

Adding the Power of Alternatives to Your Portfolio

Chapter 1 discussed the growth of mutual funds and hedge funds. It showed that hedge funds and other alternative asset classes experienced exceptional growth in the 20-year span that began in 1990 and that most of this growth was focused on a relatively narrow group of ultra-high-net-worth individuals, family offices, endowments, and foundations. One of the principal attractive aspects of hedge funds is their general lack of correlation with the two major asset classes of stocks and bonds. One characteristic of most hedge fund investors is that they have always been focused on each investment's return and risk contributions to an overall portfolio rather than focusing solely on the return of each individual investment. In the most recent years, virtually all investors now subscribe to the merits of modern portfolio theory (MPT), in which investors focus on, in addition to each investment's return and volatility, the covariance of investment with one another. In "MPT-speak," an *optimal* portfolio is one that delivers the lowest level of volatility for a given level of return or, conversely, the highest level of return for a given level of volatility.

Early hedge fund investors were aware of the uses (and limitations) of MPT, but the great majority of other investors relied on more simplified methods of portfolio construction. Most financial advisors increasingly counseled their clients, for example, to hold a diversified mix of both stocks and bonds in their portfolios. In the world of mutual funds, a balanced portfolio was taken literally, and Figure 1-4 showed that hybrid funds (initially called *bond and income funds* by the Investment Company Institute) were a recognized substrategy from 1984 onward. Hybrid funds have never accounted for more than about 7.5 percent of industry total net assets, however.

Style-Box Investing

For investors focusing on portfolios of mutual funds, a very popular form of achieving diversification was the *Style Box*. Morningstar trademarked the Style Box in 1992, and it is, in its simplest form, a nine-square grid that categorizes mutual funds by their manager's investment style and other metrics such as the manager's capitalization focus (i.e., large cap, mid cap, or small cap). Its popularity rested with its simplicity because equity mutual funds were classified, for example, with a manager's investment style on one axis and the manager's capitalization focus

FIGURE 4-1   Morningstar's Style Box

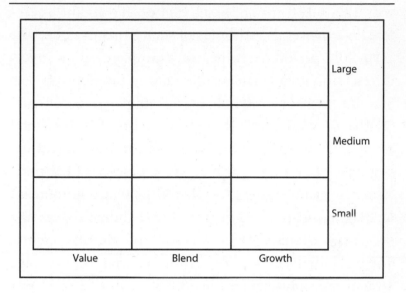

on the other axis (Figure 4-1). The Style Box has severe limitations, however, because each asset class, equities, for example, can be displayed by investment style and capitalization focus, but it does not allow for other asset classes, bonds, for example, to be included in the analysis. Bonds also can be deconstructed, of course, by two appropriate characteristics, but this has limited value. The Style Box loses further luster when investors start using non-U.S. or global sources of return in their portfolios.

Constructing a 60:40 Portfolio

One of oldest tenets of investing is the concept of achieving a 60:40 mix of equities and bonds in order to have a well-diversified portfolio. While it is unclear where this came from, many asset-allocation studies start with this 60:40 mix of asset classes. It's useful, therefore, to explore the attributes of such a mix over, say, the 1990–2012 period. Assume, for example, that an investor has only two assets available for a portfolio: (1) the Standard & Poor's 500 Index (S&P 500, total return) and (2) the Barclays Capital Aggregate Bond Index (total return).[1] Next, assume that the investor allocates, at the beginning of the 23-year period, 60 percent of the portfolio's investable assets to the S&P 500 and 40 percent to Barclays Capital Aggregate Bond Index. Figure 4-2 presents various statistical results of the investment. The first line shows, for example, that the average annual rate of return for the S&P 500 for the period was 8.55 percent, and its annual volatility was 15.01 percent. The second line shows the same statistics for the Barclays Capital Aggregate Bond Index, an annual rate of return of 6.90 percent and annual volatility of 3.70 percent.

FIGURE 4-2 Average annual rates of return, annual volatility, and Sharpe ratios for a portfolio (January 1990–December 2012, percentages)

Index/Portfolio	Average Annual Rate of Return	Annual Volatility	Sharpe Ratio
S&P 500 (TR)	8.55	15.01	0.33
Barclays Capital Aggregate Bond (TR)	6.90	3.70	0.90
60% S&P 500: 40% Barcap Agg.	8.17	12.03	0.38
10% S&P: 90% Barcap Agg.	7.23	4.74	0.76
5% S&P: 95% Barcap Agg.	7.07	3.93	0.89
4% S&P: 96% Barcap Agg.	7.04	3.81	0.90
3% S&P: 97% Barcap Agg.	7.01	3.73	0.92
2% S&P: 98% Barcap Agg.	6.97	3.68	0.92
1% S&P: 99% Barcap Agg.	6.94	3.67	0.91

Sources: Morningstar and Forward.

Because the S&P 500 and the Barclays Capital Aggregate Bond Index are not perfectly correlated with one another, combining them in a portfolio produces a more efficient result (i.e., more return for any given level of volatility or less volatility for any given level of return).

The third line in Figure 4-2 shows the results of weighting a portfolio at the beginning of the period with a 60 percent allocation to equities (the S&P 500) and a 40 percent allocation to fixed-income securities (the Barclays Capital Aggregate Bond Index). To keep things simple, this example has a single allocation period at the beginning of the 23-year period. It produces an average annual return of 8.17 percent and annual volatility of 12.03 percent.[2]

What Is a Sharpe Ratio?

Why is this result better than the 100 percent allocation to the S&P 500? Researchers calculate a measure called the *Sharpe ratio* for the portfolio by dividing an excess return statistic by the return stream's standard deviation. The Sharpe ratio (named after William Forsyth Sharpe) measures the excess return (or risk premium) per unit of deviation or risk. In other words, it is a measure of the performance of an investment computed by dividing the investment's excess return by the amount of risk taken to generate the excess return.

Looking at Figure 4-2, it's clear that the 100 percent allocation to fixed-income securities has a substantially higher Sharpe ratio than the 60:40 blended portfolio.

Moreover, the same figure also shows that a 10 percent allocation to the S&P 500 and a 90 percent allocation to the Barclays Aggregate produce a Sharpe ratio that is superior to the 60:40 blended version. In fact, a 5 percent allocation to the S&P 500 and a 95 percent to the Barclays Aggregate is better than a 10:90 allocation. The figure shows that improvement in the Sharpe ratio continues on until a 2 or 3 percent allocation to the equity index and a 98 or 97 percent allocation to fixed income index.

Is this result surprising? Well, not really. The investment period covers 1990–2012, and this 23-year span is one of the longest, if not the longest, bull-market period for bonds in U.S. history. The implications of this is that someone with perfect foresight would have created an optimal two-asset portfolio by allocating virtually all of his or her investable assets to bonds and only 2 or 3 percent to equities. The investor would have had to make this decision, of course, in the latter part of 1989, and the investor would have had to stick with the allocation for 23 years. Is this realistic? Probably not, but it demonstrates a methodology for evaluating portfolios over time that does not rely too heavily on any one person's or group's judgment of the merits of portfolios. In short, it is a useful tool but only a tool.

Mean-Variance Optimization

As discussed earlier, MPT is a theory of finance that attempts to maximize portfolio expected return for a given amount of portfolio risk or, equivalently, minimize risk for a given level of expected return. MPT was initially considered to be an important advance in the mathematical modeling of finance, but since then, many theoretical and practical criticisms have been leveled against it. Many of the underlying assumptions of MPT have been challenged by academicians and other researchers, such as that most financial return streams are not normally distributed or that correlations between asset classes are not fixed. This latter point is especially true when financial markets meet highly turbulent conditions. More recent criticism of MPT focuses on an area broadly called *behavioral economics*, and a major tenet of this work is that investors (and people, more broadly) are not rational and markets are not efficient.

Despite these shortcomings, the underlying principles of MPT are still useful in constructing a portfolio. Investors have limited time and information to make allocation decisions, and virtually all investors agree that one is probably better off if one owns a broadly diversified portfolio of assets rather than "putting all one's eggs in a basket." So how does an individual investor go about deciding which, if any, Investment Company Act of 1940 ('40 Act) alternative vehicles he or she wants to include in his or her portfolio? This is not an easy question to answer. Ultra-high-net-worth individuals, family offices, endowments, and foundations all have investment advisors that spend a great deal of time and effort in arriving at their investment decisions. Most mass-affluent investors are typically limited to their financial advisor(s), accountants, lawyers, and other individuals who may or may not have expertise in this area. Nevertheless, '40 Act alternatives are, ultimately, mutual funds, so there is information available from the usual sources, although the knowledge needed to make the best decisions may not be too widespread.

Building Customized Funds of Hedge Funds

I joined Graystone Research at Morgan Stanley in April 2001. Graystone was originally called *Graystone Partners* and was acquired by Morgan Stanley in early 2000. The three partners that started Graystone in Chicago decided to form a firm to meet the consulting needs of ultra-high-net-worth individuals and family offices in 1993. Graystone Partners advised its clients about traditional stock and bond investment managers, but it was an early strong proponent of hedge funds and made allocations to many of the oldest and most successful hedge fund firms. Shortly after I joined Morgan Stanley, the person I reported to asked me to have the Graystone team focus solely on hedge funds and other alternative investment vehicles because Morgan Stanley had other teams of individuals who were highly skilled at selecting and monitoring "traditional" stock and bond investment managers.

As briefly discussed in the Preface, the role of Graystone Research was to (1) identify, research, and monitor hedge fund and funds of hedge fund vehicles that were appropriate candidates for either one-off allocations by clients with considerable investable assets and/or (2) create customized portfolios of hedge funds that were tailored to the individual needs of clients. Members of the analyst team was located in London, New York, Chicago, and Hong Kong because hedge funds were quickly becoming a global phenomenon in financial markets. Team members in the United States specialized in one or two hedge fund substrategies, whereas the non-U.S. analysts were mostly generalists and covered a wider variety of investment styles.

The analyst team was tasked with identifying new hedge fund programs, conducting due diligence on their investment process, determining whether they were "best of breed" vehicles, and monitoring their results to ensure that they remained the best possible choices. Not surprisingly, the team had a process that required all potential new and existing managers to be reviewed first by the team and then reapproved by a committee of senior Morgan Stanley representatives. In addition, the team had other individuals charged with conducting *operational* due diligence on each manager because it is well known in "hedge fund land" that more problems arise from back-office and other operational issues than from the investment programs. These individuals had, by the way, a veto power to remove managers if they thought there was some sort of potential issue in the hedge fund organization regardless of how good the manager's track record was.

Because Graystone Research typically had about 75 to 90 hedge fund vehicles from various substrategies on the "recommended" list, the next task was to assemble them into a portfolio that reflected each client's preferences and needs. As mentioned in the Preface, the Graystone team created the first factor model to assess the individual vehicles, and the head of portfolio selection created a systematic approach that identified the optimal hedge funds given certain constraints, such as the client's proclivity for bearing risk. Graystone Research was very successful for Morgan Stanley clients, and many of the team members remain at Morgan Stanley or work in the alternative investment industry at other well-regarded firms.

After I left Morgan Stanley, the firm elected to move the Graystone Research team to Morgan Stanley Investment Management and combine it with the firm's other (and larger) hedge fund due-diligence group. Morgan Stanley owned the Graystone name, and it was going to discontinue using it when individuals in the Smith Barney Consulting Group asked to take the name, arguing that it had a very strong brand presence in the marketplace. I am happy to report that the Graystone name lives on in this new capacity.

Choosing '40 Act Alternatives

The first thing an individual investor should do is to assess his or her current portfolio and its recent results. All investors know that the investment climate has been a difficult one over the past 5 to 10 years, and most investors believe that their portfolios performed poorly. Therefore, investors need to ask themselves whether (1) their current portfolio of investments is likely to achieve their investment goals and (2) whether adding one or more alternative investment vehicles will improve the likelihood of success. This is, I believe, a much more difficult task than most people realize. Many people rely heavily on financial advisors, and the depth of knowledge about alternative investment vehicles may not be sufficient for these advisors to respond to this question.

The place to start is to review your investment history over the past few years. Has your portfolio performed in a manner that is acceptable, and are you in the process of achieving your goals? Is your portfolio positioned such that it will sufficiently weather an adverse market environment such as 2007–2008? Can you identify core holdings in your portfolio that will be able to operate in any economic and financial environment? I doubt that many people can honestly answer yes to all three of these questions. However, becoming more knowledgeable about alternative investment styles, programs, and vehicles is a great initial step. Knowing the right questions to ask is the first task that you will need to accomplish in order for you to be able to make or contribute to making the decisions necessary to build a robust all-weather portfolio.

Although this will be discussed further in Chapter 9 it's likely that most individuals' quest of constructing an all-weather portfolio will need to encompass traditional stock and bond investment companies (including exchange-traded funds), managed futures, and perhaps diversified commodity funds, real estate, and alternative investment vehicles such as '40 Act alternatives or hedge funds. Most researchers and knowledgeable market practitioners do not advocate an alternatives-only portfolio because it does not produce alpha on a consistent basis, so having a mix of vehicles is an optimal strategy.

5

Hedge Fund Performance: How Good Has It Been?

The financial media have focused heavily on the hedge fund industry for the last decade or so, and like many obsessions, it has distorted both the good and the bad. Because hedge funds do not have to resister with the Securities and Exchange Commission (SEC), there have been a number of well-publicized frauds by hedge fund investment managers and promoters. On the other side of the coin, there has been an abundance of stories touting the fabulous returns that certain hedge fund managers have achieved for themselves and their investors. As with most things, the truth is usually somewhere in the middle, so it's useful to try to put the hedge fund industry's investment performance into perspective.

Overall Picture of Hedge Fund Performance

Chapter 2 indicated that Hedge Fund Research (HFR) began publishing peer-group indexes of hedge fund monthly performance from January 1990 onward. Its principal hedge fund industry performance measure, the *Hedge Fund Research Indices (HFRI) Fund Weighted Composite Index*, is an industry average of all hedge funds that report data to HFR on a monthly basis. There is, of course, no requirement for a hedge fund investment manager to make his or her vehicle's performance information available to HFR, but almost all hedge funds report their results to one or more index providers so that investors can assess their results relative to other hedge funds. Figure 1-5 shows that the HFR database consisted of 530 hedge funds as of December 31, 1990, and this grew to 7,940 funds by December 31, 2012. Most academicians and other researchers agree that these voluntary databases have a number of flaws in their construction methodology, with features such as survivorship bias and other imperfections overstating somewhat the actual returns achieved by the hedge fund industry. Nevertheless, Chapter 2 indicated that all indexes have certain biases, and various researchers have shown that while the overstatement of, say, the industry's average annual rate of return is statistically significant, it is not so large that the index results should be rejected.

Using monthly returns, Figure 5-1 presents the average annual rate of return, average annual volatility, and Sharpe ratio for the HFRI Fund Weighted Composite Index from January 1990 through December 2012. Also shown in the figure are the same statistics for the

FIGURE 5-1   Average annual rate of return, standard deviation, and Sharpe ratio for selected indexes (monthly data; percentages)

Index	Average Annual Rate of Return	Annual Stadard Deviation	Sharpe Ratio
HFRI Fund Weighted Composite	11.93	6.36	0.70
S&P 500	8.55	15.04	0.33
Barclays Aggregate Bond	6.90	3.71	0.90

Sources: Hedge Fund Research, Morningstar, and Forward.

Standard & Poor's 500 Index (S&P 500) and the Barclays Aggregate Bond Index. The HFRI Fund Weighted Composite Index (onshore version) achieved an average annual rate of return of 11.93 percent over the 23-year period with an average annual volatility of 6.36 percent. Using the 91-day U.S. Treasury bill rate as a riskless rate of return, the HFRI Index posted a Sharpe ratio of 0.70. Figure 5-1 shows that the average return of the hedge fund index was sizably above the average return of the S&P 500, and its average annual volatility was less than half that of the S&P 500. This low level of volatility reflects the investment objective of most hedge fund portfolio managers because they attempt to manage their portfolios in a much more risk-controlled manner than long-only managers. As a result, the Sharpe ratio of the HFRI Index is considerably above the Sharpe ratio of the S&P 500. Figure 5-1 also shows that while the average annual rate of return of the Barclays Aggregate Bond Index is below the average return of both the other indexes, it was considerably less volatile than either of them as well. Accordingly, the Sharpe ratio for the fixed-income index

is appreciably higher than the Sharpe ratios for the HFRI
Index and the S&P 500.

Are Hedge Funds Worth Their Fees?

Figure 5-1 makes a strong case for the overall
investment-management capability of hedge fund portfolio managers. Their average annual returns, annual
standard deviations, and Sharpe ratios are especially
impressive in the decade of the 1990s. Figure 5-2 present
the data for the HFRI Fund Weighted Composite Index,
the S&P 500 Index, and the Barclays U.S. Aggregate
Bond Index divided into five-year subperiods. Recall
from Figure 1-2 that the decade of the 1990s was a period
of strong stock market returns, although it was accompanied by heightened volatility. Focusing on hedge fund
returns, Figure 5-2 shows hedge funds earning midteen
returns over the decade, accompanied by volatility that
was about three-fifths the volatility of the S&P 500.
This strong investment performance is reinforced by the
industry's Sharpe ratio because it averaged 1.47 over the
10-year span. This compares with the Sharpe ratio of
the S&P 500, which averaged a respectable 0.94 over the
decade. The Sharpe ratio of both equities, as measured
by the S&P 500, and the HFRI Index were moderately
better than that of the Barclays Aggregate, which averaged 0.63 over the period.

As the period shifts to the first five years of the new
millennium, however, the case for hedge funds begins to

FIGURE 5-2 Average annual rate of return, annual standard deviation, and Sharpe ratio for selected indexes (monthly data; percentages)

Period	HFRI Fund Weighted Composite			S&P 500			Barclays U.S. Aggregate Bond		
	Av. Ann. RoR	Av. Std. Deviation	Sharpe Ratio	Av. Ann. RoR	Av. Std. Deviation	Sharpe Ratio	Av. Ann. RoR	Av. Std. Deviation	Sharpe Ratio
1990–1994	18.39	7.11	1.80	8.70	12.52	0.29	7.66	4.09	0.63
1995–1999	14.98	8.08	1.14	28.56	13.95	1.59	7.73	3.74	0.63
2000–2004	6.90	5.91	0.67	–2.30	16.35	–0.30	7.71	3.96	1.20
2005–2009	5.86	7.49	0.38	0.42	16.05	–0.15	4.97	3.70	0.53
2010–2012	2.73	6.00	0.44	10.87	15.30	0.70	6.19	2.42	2.52

Sources: Hedge Fund Research, Morningstar and Forward.

erode somewhat. The HFRI Fund Weighted Composite Index achieved an average annual rate of return of 6.90 percent over the 2000–2004 period, and its average annual volatility edged down to 5.91 percent, but the Sharpe ratio tumbled to 0.67. Recall that equity prices reached a then-historic high in early 2000 but then dropped sharply over most of 2000, 2001, and 2002 as equity-market participants responded to the "popping" of the dot-com bubble. Figure 5-2 shows that the average annual rate of return for the S&P 500 was negative, at –2.30 percent, whereas volatility rose to 16.35 percent. Bonds were the clear winner over this five-year span because the Barclays Aggregate maintained a 7.71 percent return with 3.96 percent volatility and a Sharpe ratio of 1.20.

The "Great Recession"

It's always easy to identify bubbles in hindsight, and the unsustainable increase in U.S. housing prices over the mid-2000 years is no exception. Academicians and other researchers are still analyzing and debating the causes and impacts of the "great recession," but few would argue that it had a chilling effect on almost all market participants. The data presented for the five-year span 2005–2009 fail to capture the 55.96 percent drawdown in the S&P 500 from October 9, 2007, until March 9, 2009, because Figure 5-2 shows the latter half of the decade as posting an average annual rate of return of 0.42 percent with average annual volatility of 16.05 percent. As a result, U.S. equities, as measured by the S&P 500, earned an average annual rate of return of 5.86 percent, annual volatility of 7.49 percent, and a Sharpe ratio of 0.38 percent. The Barclays U.S. Aggregate Bond Index earned, on the other hand, a 4.97 percent average annual rate of return with average annual volatility for the five-year span of 3.70 percent and a Sharpe ratio of 0.53. The ability of the bond index to do relatively well over this period largely reflects the "flight to quality" that caused U.S. government-guaranteed interest rates to continue the bull-market run that began in the early 1980s. Mortgage-backed and lower-rated corporate bonds had a much more difficult time, but the rise in U.S. Treasury prices won the day for the fixed-income markets.

Will Hedge Fund Performance Recover?

The final row of data in Figure 5-2 presents the results for the three-year period ending December 31, 2012. Admittedly, these statistics use only 36 monthly observations rather than the 60 monthly observations in the other rows, but it is worth discussing the results and their possible implications. First, U.S. equities, as measured by the S&P 500, achieved a 10.87 percent average annual return, second only in size to the 28.56 percent return over the 1995–1999 span. Moreover, the average annual volatility was 15.30 percent, which is only four-fifths the S&P 500's average annual volatility over its 87-year history (see Figure 1-2). Next, the Barclays U.S. Aggregate Bond Index earned a 6.19 percent average annual return over the three years, and this occurred with volatility averaging only 2.42 percent per year. Hedge funds tallied, on the other hand, a return of only 2.73 percent, although this was achieved with a relatively low average annual volatility of 6.00 percent per year. The low return, however, resulted in a Sharpe ratio of only 0.44.

It's certainly a fair question to ask whether hedge funds, as a group, have lost their performance edge? In order to answer this question, it's useful to take a more thorough look at the hedge fund data. Figure 5-3 shows HFRI Hedge Fund Index data with the hedge funds distributed into the four major HFR substrategies: equity hedge, macro, event driven, and relative value. In a manner similar to Figure 5-2, the data are grouped into the four five-year periods that began in January 1990 and ended in December 2009 plus the three-year span ending in December 2012. These data reinforce the idea that hedge fund performance for each of the substrategies was exceptionally strong in the 1990s because virtually all the five-year periods show double-digit returns and Sharpe ratios between 1.19 and 2.46. Since January 2000, all but one of the four substrategies for each of the three time periods have produced single-digit rates of return, and the equity hedge and macro groups have achieved relatively low but still positive Sharpe ratios.

Looking at the entire 23-year period, we know that (1) equities performed well in the 1990s but poorly in

FIGURE 5-3   Selected performance statistics for hedge funds distributed by major substrategies (monthly data; percentages)

Period	Equity Hedge			Macro			Event Driven			Relative Value		
	Av. Ann. RoR	Ann. Std. Deviation	Sharpe Ratio	Av. Ann. RoR	Ann. Std. Deviation	Sharpe Ratio	Av. Ann. RoR	Ann. Std. Deviation	Sharpe Ratio	Av. Ann. RoR	Ann. Std. Deviation	Sharpe Ratio
1990–1994	20.63	7.73	1.93	25.23	10.15	1.90	15.54	6.53	1.54	15.89	4.24	2.46
1995–1999	26.92	9.54	2.16	15.97	8.18	1.25	19.08	6.91	1.90	10.56	6.36	1.19
2000–2004	6.26	8.75	0.38	8.27	6.08	0.87	10.56	6.36	1.19	8.57	2.01	2.79
2005–2009	4.53	9.71	0.16	7.02	4.95	0.80	8.57	2.01	2.79	6.00	6.36	0.47
2010–2012	2.82	8.91	0.31	1.16	5.06	0.21	5.61	6.03	0.91	7.27	3.49	2.05

Sources: Hedge Fund Research, Morningstar, and Forward.

the 2000s and (2) bonds generally performed well over the entire span. We also know that the number of hedge funds expanded rapidly over most of the period and that the total net assets of hedge funds grew significantly. It seems reasonable to assert, therefore, that portfolio managers of hedge funds are facing increasing performance headwinds as time passes. The ability to perform well and attract funds from investors was much easier when the hedge fund field was less crowded. In addition, it is much more difficult for hedge funds to attract and retain the assets of ultra-high-net-worth individuals, endowments, and foundations when the vehicles charge the typical hedge fund fees of 2 percent to manage assets while keeping 20 percent of gains (above a high-water mark) when returns are well below those of previous periods. This does not to say that there are no hedge funds worth allocating to these days because a number of hedge funds have been able to earn returns in recent years that are similar to the returns they earned 15 years ago. However, the total net assets of hedge funds are getting increasingly concentrated in the vehicles of relatively few well-known managers, whereas an increasing number of hedge funds are electing to return all or some of their capital to investors.

Hedge Funds in a Low-Return Environment

A large number of academicians and market researchers have asserted that financial-market returns are likely to be lower in the first few decades of the current century than they were in the second half of the twentieth century. This is a fairly easy prediction to make for fixed-income securities because global interest rates in developed markets are, for the most part, at unprecedented lows, and various central banks have instituted policies aimed at raising the rate of inflation to an "acceptable" level as a way to fight the forces of deflation. It seems likely, therefore, that fixed-income prices will be fighting the headwind of rising inflation, and this will limit the amount and character of gains in fixed-income-oriented investment strategies.

Many of these same researchers also point to the slowing of global growth owing to a wide variety of problems in developed and emerging markets, so the likelihood of China or another emerging-market economy spurring global trade seems increasingly unlikely. Innovation will continue to play an important role, but the likelihood of global corporations enjoying strong growth in sales and earnings is diminished. As a result, the returns available to equity-market participants may well be lower in the first two or three decades of the current millennium than in previous decades.

Investors can and will adapt to these lower returns, but the investment environment is shifting its focus to investment vehicles that offer lower fees while being less volatile in an increasingly uncertain economic and financial environment. Data on the total net assets of hedge funds suggest that the bulk of net new allocations is flowing to the larger funds with better-known managers. It seems likely, therefore, that the pace of new hedge fund offerings will continue to slow and that the number of hedge funds may begin to contract. HFR data indicate that nearly half of all hedge funds have less than $200 million in assets under management, and most funds have track records that are less than three years in length. Relatively high fees, coupled with low returns, greatly diminish the attractiveness of these hedge funds as viable candidates for receiving meaningful allocations from investors in upcoming years.

6

Managed Futures: Another Useful Vehicle in the Toolbox

Managed futures have historical performance characteristics that make the strategy highly relevant in a market environment of relatively low returns and generally rising asset-class correlations. The strategy has long had a reputation as an all weather investment choice—a characterization that was bolstered by managed futures' strong performance in the dot-com collapse of equity prices in 2000–2002 and during the brunt of the financial crisis in 2008. Until recently, all managed futures funds were run by commodity trading advisors (CTAs), individuals or organizations that provide advice and services related to trading in futures contracts, commodity options, and/or swaps. CTAs are regulated at the federal level in the United States through registration with the Commodity Futures Trading Commission (CFTC) and membership in the National Futures Association (NFA). The first publically available managed futures fund was introduced in 1948, but the first managed futures Investment Company Act of 1940 ('40 Act) alternatives vehicle was not offered to the public until 2007.

Futures Contract Trading

The long history of futures trading can be traced back to seventeenth-century Japan, although there is some evidence that there also may have been rice futures traded in China as long as 6,000 years ago. Trading in futures contracts is a natural outgrowth of problems associated with maintaining a year-round supply of seasonal products such as rice, wheat, or corn. In the United States, the first organized commodity exchange was the Chicago Board of Trade (CBOT), and it began operating in 1848. Like many futures contracts, the CBOT's corn contract started as a *forward* contract. Farmers in the greater Chicago area began storing their corn in warehouses along the Chicago River. Farmers were given receipts for their corn, and both farmers and commercial agents began trading these receipts.

The CBOT provided a centralized place for buyers and sellers to transact these forward contracts. A *forward contract* is a nonstandardized contract between two parties to buy or sell an asset at a specified future time at a price agreed on today. This is in contrast to a *spot contract*, which is an agreement to buy or sell an asset today. In a forward contract transaction, the party agreeing to buy the underlying asset in the future assumes a long position, and the party agreeing to sell the asset in the future assumes a short position. The price agreed on is called the *delivery price*, which is equal to the forward price at the time the contract is established.

The Role of the Chicago River

Few individuals visiting or even living in Chicago realize the historical importance of the Chicago River. The river demarks the loop area from the north side of the city, and it is an attractive waterway from Lake Michigan to about a mile west (Wolf Point), where it divides into a North and South Branch. The North Branch meanders unremarkably up through several suburban areas, including the Chicago Botanic Gardens, and is known locally as the Skokie Lagoons. The South Branch is equally unremarkable except that it eventually runs into an area named the Chicago Portage. The early European explorers Louis Joliet and Father Jacques Marquette were canoeing upstream on the Mississippi River. They were guided to the Chicago Portage by local Native Americans after paddling along the Illinois and Des Plaines Rivers. They eventually encountered a swampy area known as Mud Lake, a muddy swamplike area that connected the Des Plaines River to the Chicago River. The Native Americans knew that they could portage their canoes around Mud Lake and thereby have a route that connected the Great Lakes to the Mississippi River.

(continued)

Early Chicagoans built a canal, the Illinois and Michigan Canal, through the area, and this created a transportation waterway that eventually connected the Atlantic Ocean to the Gulf of Mexico. This mode of transportation was a principal reason that Chicago grew quickly and eventually eclipsed St. Louis as the jumping-off point to the American West. Some years after the canal was built (1900), engineers permanently reversed the flow direction of the Chicago River, and to this day, it flows out of Lake Michigan, not into Lake Michigan.

The CBOT's forward contracts morphed into futures contracts in 1864. A *futures contract* has all of the aspects of a forward contract but also standardizes the specific good (amount, quality, etc.) and delivery period for the contract. The CBOT initially used a *ring system* for clearing trades among CBOT members, but this eventually gave way to an independent clearinghouse, where all counterparty risk was guaranteed by the clearinghouse.[1]

Growth of CTAs and Managed Futures Mutual Funds

Just as certain index providers, such as Hedge Fund Research, collected data on the total net assets of hedge funds, other groups focused on measuring the performance and total net assets of CTAs. Barclay Hedge is

FIGURE 6-1   Managed futures total net assets (billions of dollars)

Year-end	CTA's	Mutual Funds
1980	0.30	–
1985	1.50	–
1990	10.50	–
1995	22.80	–
2000	37.90	–
2001	41.30	–
2002	50.90	–
2003	86.50	–
2004	131.90	–
2005	130.60	–
2006	170.00	–
2007	206.60	0.20
2008	206.40	1.30
2009	213.60	2.40
2010	267.60	4.40
2011	314.30	9.10
2012	329.60	9.20

Sources: CTAs: Barclay Hedge; mutual funds: Strategic Insight.

one such group. Figure 6-1 presents the total net assets of CTAs from 1980 through 2012 (five-year intervals to 2000 and annually thereafter). After a negligible amount of assets in 1980, the asset class more than tripled from 1990 through 2000 and then, with the exception of 2005 and 2008, grew strongly over the next 12 years to total net assets of $329.6 billion at year-end 2012.

What explains this remarkable growth? More and more investors came to realize the potential of managed futures as an asset that, over full market cycles, has produced strong, equity like returns and is an excellent portfolio diversifier. Over the 32-year period ending

FIGURE 6-2   Returns, volatilities, maximum drawdowns, and correlation coefficients for selected indexes (monthly data; percentages)

Index	Average Annual Rate of Return	Annual Standard Deviation	Max Monthly Drawdown	Correlation to S&P 500
Barclay CTA Index	11.16	15.07	−9.81	0.01
S&P 500 Index	11.06	15.62	−21.54	1.00
Barcap Agg. Bond Index	8.69	5.69	−5.92	0.20

Sources: Barclay Hedge, Barclays Capital, and Standard & Poor's.

December 31, 2012, Figure 6-2 shows that the Barclays CTA Index of managed futures funds achieved an average annual rate of return of 11.16 percent, comparing favorably with annualized gains of 11.06 percent for the Standard & Poor's 500 Index (S&P 500) and 8.69 percent for the Barclays Capital Aggregate U.S. Bond Index. Both the Barclays CTA Index and the S&P 500 recorded standard deviations that were quite similar, although Figure 6-2 shows that the maximum monthly decline for the S&P 500 was −21.54 percent versus −9.81 percent for the Barclays CTA Index. The final column in Figure 6-2 presents the correlation coefficients for the Barcalys CTA Index and the Barclays Aggregate U.S. Bond Index with the S&P 500. These data demonstrate that managed futures is an excellent diversifier because the asset class has virtually no correlation with U.S. equities.

One of the strongest appeals of managed futures as an asset class is how well they perform in periods when broad equity markets perform poorly. In 1992, 2002, and 2008, for example, the Barclays CTA Index recorded

FIGURE 6-3   Selected asset-class correlation matrix (January 1, 1992–December 31, 2012; monthly data)

Index	Managed Futures	Fixed Income	Commodities	Intl. Equity	EM Equity	U.S. Large Cap.	U.S. Small Cap.
Barclay CTA Index	1.00	0.23	0.18	0.02	–0.02	–0.07	–0.09
Barcap U.S. Bond	0.23	1.00	0.03	0.05	–0.04	0.06	0.04
S & P GSCI	0.18	0.03	1.00	0.35	0.33	0.24	0.29
MSCI EAFE	0.02	0.05	0.35	1.00	0.75	0.78	0.71
MSCI EM	–0.02	–0.04	0.33	0.75	1.00	0.71	0.72
S&P 500	–0.07	0.06	0.24	0.78	0.71	1.00	0.80
Russell 2000	–0.09	–0.04	0.29	0.71	0.72	0.80	1.00

Sources: Barclay Hedge, Barclays Capital, and Standard & Poor's.

double-digit gains, whereas the S&P 500 lost ground. This is the same pattern that is evident for other broad indexes as well. Figure 6-3 shows asset-class correlations for a variety of indexes over the 21-year period from January 1, 1992, through December 31, 2012. These data show very low correlations between managed futures and fixed-income vehicles, commodities, international equity, emerging-markets equity, U.S. large-cap stocks, and U.S. small-cap stocks.

As noted earlier, the earliest CTA funds only traded commodities. This reflected the fact that early U.S. futures markets focused on things that were either grown in the ground (grains, etc.), lived on the ground (feeder cattle, etc.), or were extracted from the ground (industrial metals such as copper). The role of futures markets in the first two categories was to provide a year-round market for products that had a production cycle that may or may not be different from their consumption cycle. The commodity exchanges would create delivery months for periods that facilitated the production-consumption mismatch. The focus on commodities only took a radical turn in the 1970s, when the two principal Chicago-based commodity exchanges listed contracts based on financial instruments.

Financial Futures Come to the Fore

The Chicago Mercantile Exchange (CME) listed contracts on foreign-exchange cross-rates between the U.S. dollar and several major non-U.S.-dollar currencies in 1973, and the CBOT listed the first contract based on interest rates when it began trading a contract based on Government National Mortgage Association (GNMA or Ginnie Mae)–guaranteed mortgages in 1975. The two Chicago commodity exchanges competed aggressively, and the CME next listed contracts based on three-month U.S. Treasury bills followed by contracts on three-month certificates of deposit (CDs) issued by top-quality commercial banks. Not to be outdone, the CBOT listed a futures contract based on long-term U.S. Treasury bonds in the summer of 1977.[2]

All the futures contracts up to this point were *delivery* contracts, where the contract specifications required the short position holder to deliver the specified amount and grade of the contract to the long position holder in the stated delivery process. Physical delivery requires the futures contract price to eventually meet the spot-market price, as the long contract holder receives the specified good and the short contract holder delivers it and is paid an amount depending on the final settlement price of the contract. All this changed in the first quarter of 1982, however. The CME petitioned the CFTC to permit it to trade a three-month Eurodollar contract that was *cash settled*. In the case of the CME's contract, the final settlement price was determined by a polling of the major international commercial banks located in London. The initial response to the CME's Eurodollar futures contract was tepid, but it eventually became the most widely traded futures contract around the globe.[3]

Shortly after the initiation of Eurodollar futures trading at the CME, a new, hotly contested battle emerged for dominance in stock-index futures contracts, also cash settled. The first entrant was the Kansas City Board of Trade's (KCBT's) contract based on the Value Line Stock Price Index in March 1982. The following month saw the New York Futures Exchange (NYFE), a newly formed subsidiary of the New York Stock Exchange (NYSE), list a futures contract based on the New York Stock Exchange Composite Index. Shortly thereafter, the CME listed its S&P 500 futures contract, and it quickly became the dominant instrument in the fast-growing area of stock-index futures contracts.[4]

Multiple-Asset-Class Futures Contracts

Once stock-index futures became established, futures market participants, including investment managers, had a much wider array of instruments with which to work. Investment managers of managed futures strategies could now access commodities, foreign-exchange, and interest-rate and stock-index futures in their investment programs. This made CTAs much more interested in adopting these new financial futures contracts in their programs, and it made their programs much more interesting to investors. By transforming a commodities-only-focused strategy into one with broad multiple-asset-class exposure and flexible, built-in diversification, this development began to turbocharge the growth of managed futures products.

Types of CTA Programs

Managed futures strategies may invest in more than 150 different futures markets, and all of these are listed contracts on regulated futures exchanges that offer two-way markets to investors. Broadly speaking, managed futures strategies come in two different flavors:

1. *Fundamental* (or *discretionary*) *strategies* based on a manager's analysis and judgment of factors such as supply and demand, macroeconomic indicators, and geopolitical events
2. *Systematic strategies* that employ a consistent methodology in an effort to capitalize on trends or patterns in futures pricing

Although both of these strategies are widely employed, BarclayHedge data estimate that more than 80 percent of CTA net assets are in systematic programs, and most of these use a trend-following approach. All five of the largest CTA programs at the end of 2011 were trend-following programs, and 7 of the top 10 were trend following.[5]

Trend-following strategies generally refrain from trying to predict market trends. Rather, they aim to identify trends that have enough scale or persistence to give investment managers the opportunity to generate a profit after all costs are taken into account. Most investment managers who employ trend-following strategies operate by using various algorithms to signal when to buy or sell individual futures contracts, based, in most instances, on a time series of futures contract prices. These types of programs do not qualify as a passive approach because they do not mirror an index. Instead, investment managers aim to identify trends based on moving averages, channel breakouts, exponential smoothing techniques, or any number of other quantitative factors. Trend-following systems necessarily have at least three components: (1) an algorithm to identify the trend, (2) a methodology for capitalizing on it, and (3) an algorithm to identify when the trend has run its course and a position should be exited.

Managers who use trend-following strategies often initiate a large number of positions with the expectation that a majority of them will be exited at no loss (a *scratch trade*) or at a small loss relative to the capital being employed. If a large number of trend-following signals are executed but result in relatively small losses, then the manager using this approach may have what is known as a *low batting average*. However, the manager can still have a profitable overall program if winning positions more than offset the losses from the losing positions.

Why Do Markets Trend?

Despite the popularity of trend-following strategies and 50+ years of studies on the informational content of security-price time series, the approach is far from being universally embraced. Academicians and other researchers who subscribe to various forms of the *random-walk theory* of financial market prices maintain that the patterns of past securities prices have little or no bearing on subsequent prices. Notwithstanding the continuing debate on this topic over the last 20 years or so, a growing body of literature has been published to support the notion that securities prices can have identifiable periods of sustained momentum. A 2007 literature survey concluded that 56 of 90 modern studies mostly supported the validity of technical analysis.[6] Research also has demonstrated that virtually all managed futures programs have return patterns with a high correlation with relatively simple trend-following models.[7]

Even if we accept the premise that markets do trend, it is reasonable to ask why. Researchers have offered varied explanations, but once again, no one answer is widely accepted as definitive. Perhaps the most commonly posited cause is that investors tend to underreact to new information, causing new price estimates to remain somewhat tethered to old prices, and to overreact once new information is widely distributed. More investors hop on board as the trend is established, further extending the trend. Ultimately, as market conditions change, trends inevitably become overextended and begin slowing appreciably or reversing direction. This behavioral explanation implies that investors are less rational than many market theories assume, a conclusion reached by a number of behavioral economists.[8]

What Do Managed Futures Bring to Portfolios?

As noted earlier, CTA investment programs historically have demonstrated the ability to produce equity-like returns with low correlations with equities and, to a lesser extent, bonds. The full benefits of these characteristics become apparent when managed futures are added to a traditional stock and bond portfolio.

As a basis for comparison, let's begin with a portfolio constructed, as we did in Chapter 4, with an allocation of 60 percent to U.S. stocks (as measured by the S&P 500) and 40 percent to bonds (as measured by the Barclays Aggregate U.S. Bond Index). We know from Chapter 4 that combining them will produce a portfolio that is more efficient than either asset class alone in terms of its ability to produce risk-adjusted return, as measured by the Sharpe ratio. Indeed, we saw in Chapter 4 that this two-asset class would have produced an annual return of 8.17 percent, with an average annual standard deviation of 12.03 percent and a Sharpe ratio of 0.37 for the 23-year period ending December 31, 2012.

When managed futures, as measured by the BarclayHedge CTA Index, are substituted for a portion of the equity allocation, Figure 6-4 shows that the portfolio's performance improves. Figure 6-4 adds an allocation to CTAs in 5 percent intervals—that is, starting at a 5 percent allocation and then increasing it by 5 percent to a total managed futures allocation of 10, 15, and 20 percent, respectively. The figure shows that the average annual rate of return decreased to 8.14 percent over the 23-year period, but its annual average standard deviation dropped to 11.82 percent, and its Sharpe ratio climbed to 0.38. The same figure shows further improvements as the CTA Index allocation is increased to 10, 15, and 20 percent, respectively. The improvements in the Sharpe ratio when the CTA allocation is boosted are, admittedly, small, but the process added only a small

FIGURE 6-4   Returns, volatility, and Sharpe ratios for selected portfolios (January 1990–December 2012; monthly data)

Portfolio Combination	Avg. Annual Rate of Return	Avg. Annual Standard Deviation	Sharpe Ratio
60% S&P 500: 40% BarCap Agg	8.17%	12.03%	0.37
55% S&P 500: 40% BarCap Agg: 5% Barclay CTA	8.14	11.82	0.38
50% S&P 500: 40% BarCap Agg: 10% Barclay CTA	8.11	11.59	0.39
45% S&P 500: 40% BarCap Agg: 15% Barclay CTA	8.07	11.32	0.39
40% S&P 500: 40% BarCap Agg: 20% Barclay CTA	8.03	10.99	0.40

Sources: Morningstar and Forward.

number of managed futures to the asset mix, and the changes produced consistent results.

A number of academic and other research studies support the notion that adding managed futures to a traditional portfolio may improve its risk-adjusted returns owing to, in large part, the low correlations between managed futures and other asset classes. An early proponent of this view was Harvard Professor John Lintner, who authored a seminal paper on the topic in 1983.[9] Similar conclusions were reported in the *Journal of Investment Management* in 2004[10] and in an Ibbotson Associates study released in 2005.[11] A 2009 study sponsored by the Chicago Board Options Exchange (CBOE) explored the impacts of the 2008 financial crisis on investment portfolios and found that as other asset classes became more correlated during the crisis, managed futures became less so.[12]

There are, of course, no guarantees that managed futures will remain uncorrelated with other asset classes in the future. In the meantime, though, historical evidence suggests that diversifying with managed futures may be one way that investors can achieve better returns for the same level of risk or lower risk for a given level of return.

Managed Futures Mutual Funds Enter the Stage

For many years, CTAs were the only vehicles through which investors could access managed futures strategies. The strategy became considerably more accessible, however, when the first managed futures mutual fund was offered to investors in 2007, and Chapter 3 indicated that the number of managed futures vehicles had risen to 48 with total net assets of $9.6 billion as of December 31, 2012. Similar to CTAs, managed futures mutual funds overwhelmingly use some sort of trend-following or momentum strategy according to the Morningstar database of '40 Act alternatives. More than half the vehicles employ strategies that were developed specifically for the mutual fund, whereas another third is organized as funds of funds, where the mutual fund investment manager selects and monitors other funds, typically CTAs, in a multifund structure.

It is important to recognize, however, that CTAs and managed futures mutual funds have a number of differences. CTAs are generally open, in a manner similar to hedge funds, to *accredited* or *qualified* investors only. Accordingly, as of September 30, 2011, the median required initial investment was $250,000 for single-manager managed futures CTAs in Morningstar's database and $50,000 for the median fund of hedge funds.[13] Morningstar does note, however, that a few registered commodity pools require minimum investments of as little as $1,000. In contrast, managed futures mutual funds have no qualification hurdle for investors; the median minimum investment is only $2,500.

In the area of fees, CTAs typically operate with a hedge fund–like fee structure that combines an asset-management fee with a performance fee, the latter of which is generally subject to a high-water mark.

The median fees for hedge funds employing managed futures strategies are a 2 percent management fee and a 20 percent performance fee. Hedge fund of funds managers typically charge a 1.5 percent management fee and a 10 percent performance fee on top of the underlying fees of the CTA or hedge fund.

Management fees charged by managed futures mutual funds are mostly in the 1 to 2 percent range, and most do not have performance fees. As with all mutual funds, a managed futures mutual fund must publish all or most of its operating expenses, and these typically average about 2 percent. Unfortunately, data are not readily available on the expenses charged by hedge funds and CTAs, but they are likely to be at least 1 percent per year, if not more.

Since the U.S. Congress amended, in 1974, the Commodity Exchange Act of 1936, all CTAs have been regulated the Commodities Futures Trading Commission (CFTC). They must also register with the National Futures Association (NFA), the industry's self-regulatory group. Additionally, all account representatives who transact for clients in futures and options must successfully pass the CFTC's Series 3 examination. Lastly, a Series 31 test is required for individuals who wish to receive trailing commissions on commodity limited partnerships, commodity pools, or managed accounts guided by CTAs. The Series 31 license is also meant for those supervising these same limited activities. Individuals who take this exam in lieu of the Series 3 test cannot open individual futures trading accounts. A prerequisite is registration with the Financial Industry Regulatory Authority (FINRA), usually via the Series 7 exam.

With the passage of new CFTC rules in February 2012, all managed futures mutual funds are now required to register with the CFTC as *commodity pool operators* (CPOs), and they remain subject to regulation by the Securities and Exchange Commission (SEC) and FINRA. Lastly, on August 13, 2013, the CFTC issued final rules clarifying the compliance obligations for investment advisors of registered investment companies, who must register with the CFTC as CPOs.

Conclusion

With correlations rising among and within asset classes, geographic diversification may no longer be sufficient to allow investors to reduce portfolio risk. Investors seeking new and potentially more effective ways of diversifying may wish to consider adding managed futures to their portfolios, given the strategy's track record of low correlations coupled with upside return potential. The introduction of managed futures mutual funds as one style of the new breed of '40 Act alternatives has made this option more accessible while lowering fees and providing daily liquidity and enhanced transparency relative to limited-partnership vehicles such as CTAs.

7

Performance History
of Liquid Alternatives

everal of the previous chapters, especially Chapter 5,
dealt with the performance history of hedge funds.
Chapter 5 showed, for example, that the performance of
hedge funds, as measured by the Hedge Fund Research
Indices (HFRI) Fund Weighted Composite Index, was
especially strong in the 1990s and early 2000s, but recent
performance has been less extraordinary, even disap-
pointing. Proponents of hedge funds argue that the
return streams from all asset classes have been lower
over the past decade, and hedge fund managers are
mostly delivering return streams that are acceptably
positive with less volatility than traditional long-only
managers.

This is the subject, however, of ongoing debate.
Evidence presented in earlier chapters documents the
lower level of both equity and bond returns over, say, the
last 10 years relative to their long-run historical returns.
Moreover, a number of studies have been published in

recent years that focus on the lower level of recent stock- and bond-market returns, and these and other studies also have suggested the possibility of these lower returns becoming a permanent fixture in the investing land- scape.[1] Many of these studies conclude that investors must seek out noncorrelated, globally focused invest- ments if a long-run portfolio return of even 10 percent is going to be achieved. More recently, the 30-year bull market in U.S. fixed-income prices may be ending, and this has important consequences for bond and other fixed-income investors who have relied on price gains to bolster their overall fixed-income returns.

The recent lower-return environment around the globe has created challenges for many traditional hedge fund and other private investment company managers. The relatively high overall fees of hedge funds, private equity vehicles, and other so-called traditional alterna- tive investment funds result in after-fee returns that are less attractive to investors, both large and small. These relatively high fees have helped to create demand for Investment Company Act of 1940 ('40 Act) alternative vehicles because the fee structures of these vehicles are typically lower than the 2 and 20 percent plus operat- ing expenses fees of the traditional alternative private funds. This is an important topic, and it will receive more attention in Chapter 8. Meanwhile, the over- all performance characteristics of '40 Act alternative mutual funds needs to be documented and analyzed, and that is the focus of this chapter.

Creating Peer-Group Indexes for Liquid Alternatives

Just as Hedge Fund Research (HFR), Hennessey, and others began creating and publishing peer-group indexes on a monthly basis for hedge funds in the early 1990s, the same technique can be used to create peer-group indexes for '40 Act alternative vehicles. Mutual fund net asset values are, of course, published on a daily basis, and one can chain the daily returns together to have a monthly series that is comparable with, say, the HFRI series. As a first pass, let's look at the performance results for all the '40 Act alternatives that were in existence from January 1990 onward. We know, of course, that the liquid alternative mutual funds that existed in this period were not called *alternative* vehicles, and very few investors even were aware that hedge funds existed. As was discussed in Chapter 3, the '40 Act alternative universe can be defined in several ways, and each definition has pluses and minuses that have an impact on both the number of funds and their total net assets. Chapter 3 demonstrated that Morningstar defines the '40 Act, or liquid, alternative universe as being comprised of seven substrategies: (1) equity long/short, (2) currency, (3) nontraditional bond, (4) market neutral, (5) bear market, (6) multialternative, and (7) managed futures.

Only six of these early liquid alternative substrategies had any mutual fund vehicles so classified by Morningstar in January 1990, and the number increased to only seven vehicles in December 1990. As of January 1990, two of the vehicles were equity long/short mutual funds, two were currency vehicles, one was a nontraditional bond fund, and one was a market-neutral fund. Only one additional liquid alternative fund came into existence over the period ending December 1990, and this was a second market-neutral fund. Each of the funds recorded a monthly rate of return in each of the 12 months ending December 1990, and these monthly returns are adjusted for any dividends or capital gains that were distributed to shareholders and after all fund expenses.

An average monthly rate of return can be calculated for the first 10 months by summing each fund's monthly return and dividing this total by six. The same procedure can be used for the last two months by boosting the fund count to seven. Next, each of the monthly returns can be chained together by multiplying each of the monthly returns. This exercise produces a 1990 annual rate of return for the fledgling '40 Act alternative universe of 8.22 percent. Is this realistic? Well the Standard & Poor's 500 Index (S&P 500, on a total return basis) achieved a rate of return in 1990 of –3.10 percent, and the HFRI Fund Weighted Composite Index was 5.81 percent. Moving to 1991 and using the same methodology produce an annual rate of return for the '40 Act alternatives peer group of 15.34 percent for the eight funds that existed in December 1991 versus 30.45 percent for the S&P 500 and 32.19 percent for the HFRI Index.

The large variation in the three measures for this two-year period likely reflects a number of attributes. First, the S&P 500 is a broadly based measure of U.S. equity-stock prices, whereas both the peer-group indexes reflect the composition of the underlying strategies that comprise the investment companies in each universe. In addition, the number and total net assets of the '40 Act alternative vehicles is relatively miniscule compared with the HFRI Fund Weighted Composite Index. According to HFRI, the numbers of hedge funds in its Composite Index at the end of 1990 and the end of 1991 were 530 and 694, respectively, and their total net assets were $38.9 billion and $58.4 billion, respectively. These numbers are, of course, considerably larger than the number and total net assets of '40 Act alternative mutual funds for the same period (seven funds with total net assets of $1.0 billion in December 1990 and eight funds with assets of $1.1 billion in December 1991).

'40 Act Alternatives Performance: 1990–2012

Despite the relative paucity of '40 Act alternative mutual funds in the early 1990s, they can be aggregated into a peer-group composite index as well as subindexes to assess their performance relative to other asset-class indexes and peer-group measures. Figure 7-1 shows, for example, the annual performance of the S&P 500, the HFRI Fund Weighted Composite Index, and the '40 Act Alternatives Peer Group Index (discussed earlier) for the 23-year period from 1990 through 2012. The figure also presents summary statistics in the form of the average annual rate of return, the average annual standard deviation, and the Sharpe ratio for each of the three measures. It is noteworthy, for example, that the S&P 500 column shows only five years with negative returns, although 2008 was a decline of –37.0 percent on a total-return basis.

The second column of data in Figure 7-1 is the HFRI Fund Weighted Composite Index, and these data show

FIGURE 7-1   Average annual rates of return for selected indexes (percentages)

Year	S&P 500 Index	HFRI Fund Weighted Composite Index	'40 Act Alternatives Peer Group Index
1990	–3.10	5.81	7.52
1991	30.47	32.19	13.09
1992	7.62	21.22	5.94
1993	10.08	30.88	11.24
1994	1.32	4.10	2.48
1995	37.58	21.50	8.96
1996	22.96	21.10	5.00
1997	33.36	16.79	4.35
1998	28.58	2.62	–2.39
1999	21.04	31.29	–5.69
2000	–9.10	4.98	12.50
2001	–11.88	4.62	11.31
2002	–22.10	–1.45	12.19
2003	28.68	19.55	–1.03
2004	10.88	9.03	1.10
2005	4.91	9.30	3.15
2006	15.79	12.89	3.06
2007	5.49	9.96	2.92
2008	–37.00	–19.03	–1.67
2009	26.46	19.98	–0.41
2010	15.06	10.25	0.27
2011	2.11	–5.25	–2.15
2012	16.00	6.36	0.29
Avg. Annual Rate of Return	**8.55**	**11.93**	**3.86**
Annual Standard Deviation	**15.04**	**6.36**	**4.63**
Sharpe Ratio	**0.33**	**0.7**	**0.08**

Sources: Strategic Insights, Morningstar, and Forward.

that hedge funds, as a group, had only three negative years over the 23-year span. The index declined only once, by –1.45 percent in 2002, until the broad market selloff in 2008, when the index dropped by –19.03 percent. It was the relatively stellar performance of hedge funds over the 18 years until 2008 that fostered the perception that these vehicles were *absolute-return investments*. The average hedge fund's performance may have been better than that of the S&P 500 in 2008, but few individuals, if any, would argue that an average decline of nearly 20 percent could be considered an acceptable absolute-return result.

The final column of Figure 7-1 presents the performance results for the '40 Act Alternative Peer Group Index. These data show that annual gains were recorded in 17 of the years and annual declines in 6 of the years. Moreover, looking across the rows for the three time series shows a lack of correspondence. Only the 2008 year shows, for example, a decline by all three measures, whereas 13 years show increases in all three indexes, although several of these years show sizable differences.

The bottom three rows of Figure 7-1 present the average annual rate of return, average annual standard deviation, and the Sharpe ratio for each of the three indexes. The first cell shows that the S&P 500 achieved an average annual rate of return of 8.55 percent for the 23-year period, and the index's annual standard deviation and Sharpe ratio were 15.04 and 0.33, respectively. The second column shows that the HFRI Composite Index achieved a much higher average annual rate of return, at 11.93 percent, than the S&P 500 and that this was earned at a substantially lower standard deviation of 6.36 percent, which produced a higher Sharpe ratio of 0.70. Moving to the third set of data, the '40 Act Alternatives Peer Group Index, Figure 7-1 shows an average annual rate of return of 3.86 percent, an average annual standard deviation of 4.63 percent, and a Sharpe ratio of 0.08.

Examining the summary statistics for the three series certainly raises the issue of why the '40 Act Alternatives Peer Group Index data are below the measures for the HFRI Composite Index. To answer this question, Figure 7-2 shows the '40 Act alternatives data disaggregated into its seven major substrategies. Focusing first on the summary statistics, six of the seven substrategies show positive average annual returns (ranging from 8.71 percent for equity long/short to 0.59 percent for multi-alternative), but the bear-market substrategy produced a negative average annual rate of return of –10.73 percent. The bear-market substrategy's annual standard deviation, at 23.72 percent, is also appreciably higher than that of any of the other six substrategies. And not surprisingly, the Sharpe ratio for the category, at –0.58, is considerably weaker than the Sharpe ratios for any of the other six substrategies.

It is reasonable to ask, of course, why the bear-market substrategy has such a poor performance record. On this subject, one must examine the components of

Year	Equity Long/Short	Currency	Nontraditional Bond	Market Neutral	Bear Market	Multi-Alternative	Managed Futures
1990	5.84	15.99	8.37	-2.01	1.31	-	-
1991	16.56	11.31	18.81	15.44	-0.39	-	-
1992	9.02	4.07	11.10	8.76	-10.33	-	-
1993	9.70	7.72	10.17	14.51	12.70	-	-
1994	2.40	5.50	1.47	1.11	0.93	-	-
1995	16.40	12.20	14.35	11.92	-11.87	-	-
1996	17.70	-0.60	11.98	7.53	10.40	-	-
1997	19.96	-3.25	11.33	9.05	-17.83	-	-
1998	19.89	10.43	3.57	5.26	-33.74	-	-
1999	17.60	-8.92	4.56	8.23	-38.92	-	-
2000	10.87	-5.26	4.07	9.13	19.95	-	-
2001	4.11	0.20	6.65	10.07	17.65	-10.11	-
2002	-3.12	20.67	4.60	4.56	36.70	-23.87	-
2003	18.58	16.12	14.77	6.86	-37.54	18.00	-
2004	11.85	6.75	5.94	3.47	-16.06	8.84	-
2005	8.66	-2.27	3.17	3.92	-3.64	4.75	-
2006	9.71	6.95	6.33	8.78	-12.07	10.51	-
2007	5.53	8.27	3.81	7.61	-6.74	3.83	-
2008	-17.36	-1.54	-11.42	-1.96	41.22	-18.04	8.53
2009	16.40	5.08	21.57	4.22	49.68	15.66	0.30
2010	6.45	2.50	7.02	0.32	29.52	6.06	5.11
2011	-2.86	-2.07	0.40	1.78	-8.61	-2.57	-3.85
2012	5.06	2.59	8.37	0.86	-24.96	3.68	-5.69
Avg. Annual Rate of Return	**8.71**	**4.64**	**7.23**	**5.96**	**-10.73**	**0.59**	**1.83**
Annual Standard Deviation	**6.89**	**6.11**	**3.96**	**3.80**	**23.72**	**10.00**	**8.32**
Sharpe Ratio	**0.73**	**0.18**	**0.92**	**0.63**	**-0.58**	**-0.13**	**0.11**

Sources: Strategic Insight, Morningstar, and Forward.

the substrategy to look for clues. The first bear-market fund, as noted in Chapter 3, began operating in 1985, and the portfolio managers focused on building a portfolio of overvalued securities that they believed would likely to decline in price. The second bear-market fund, on the other hand, was started in early 1994, and this vehicle was an *inverse-index fund*. Investors in this vehicle are not relying on portfolio managers to identify overvalued companies. Instead, the vehicle is designed to give the inverse percentage change in the underlying index on any particular trading day. If the Standard & Poor's 500 Index (S&P 500) declines by, say, 2 percent on a particular day, the investor in the inverse-index fund will have a gain of approximately 2 percent for that trading session. If, on the other hand, the S&P 500 has a gain of 2 percent on the day, the fund investor will have a loss of about 2 percent for the session.

Looking at the entire 23-year period, there were 30 bear-market mutual funds as of December 2012, and approximately two-thirds of these were inverse-index funds, some of which delivered two times the inverse of the daily change in the underlying index. There are 28 bear-market funds that have a track record of at least 36 months, and none of these funds achieved, surprisingly, a positive average annual rate of return over their existence. Moreover, the number and total net assets of these funds have not grown appreciably in recent years because the investor appetite for their strategy appears to have waned.

Because all the bear-market '40 Act alternative mutual funds have recorded negative average annual rates of return over their existence, it is useful to look at a subsector of the universe of '40 Act alternative mutual funds by excluding the bear-market vehicles entirely. The first column of data in Figure 7-3 shows the entire

FIGURE 7-3   Average annual rates of return for selected '40 Act alternative peer groups (1990–2012; monthly data)

Year	'40 Act Alternatives Peer Group Index	'40 Act Alternatives Peer Group Index Minus Bear Market
1990	7.52	8.24
1991	13.09	14.89
1992	5.54	8.12
1993	11.24	10.94
1994	2.48	2.52
1995	8.96	13.60
1996	5.00	9.52
1997	4.35	10.26
1998	−2.39	10.57
1999	−5.69	9.02
2000	12.50	7.33
2001	11.31	5.23
2002	12.15	1.23
2003	−1.03	15.11
2004	1.10	8.45
2005	3.15	5.06
2006	3.06	8.84
2007	2.92	5.75
2008	−1.67	−12.35
2009	−0.41	13.57
2010	0.27	5.31
2011	−2.15	−1.67
2012	0.29	3.15
Avg. Annual Rate of Return	**3.86**	**6.90**
Annual Standard Deviation	**4.63**	**4.44**
Sharpe Ratio	**0.08**	**0.75**

Sources: Strategic Insights, Morningstar, and Forward.

universe of '40 Act alternative vehicles, and the second column lists the six substrategies without the bear-market funds. As noted earlier, the year-by-year data show six years when the average annual rate of return was negative. However, the number of negative years drops to two when the bear-market funds are excluded. Focusing on the summary statistics, removing the bear-market mutual funds boosts the average annual rate of return from 3.86 to 6.90 percent, and the average Sharpe ratio climbs from 0.08 to 0.75 (a higher Sharpe ratio than the HFRI Fund Weighted Composite Index for the same period).

Two questions about this analysis need to be answered. First, is it legitimate to remove the bear-market mutual funds and assess the '40 Act alternative universe without these vehicles? Second, should the same effort be made for the HFRI hedge funds that are classified as *short-biased managers*? The answer to the first question is "Yes" because the preponderance of these mutual funds are inverse-index strategies rather than short-biased managers. These types of mutual funds are, for the most part, more useful as tactical additions to a portfolio when the outlook becomes especially worrisome rather than strategic allocations aimed at achieving a portfolio's overall objective. With regard to the second question, the impact of short-biased hedge fund managers is considerably smaller in the hedge fund universe than in the bear-market mutual funds in the '40 Act alternative universe. In other words, it would make a better apples-to-apples comparison to remove the short-biased hedge funds, but the overall impact would be quite small.

Further Assessing the Performance of Hedge Funds versus '40 Act Alternatives

The summary statistics presented in Figure 7-3 for the '40 Act Alternative Peer Group Index (excluding the bear-market funds) show that the '40 Act alternatives average annual rate of return, at 6.90 percent for the 23-year period, is only about three-fifths of the average annual rate of return, 11.93 percent, for the HFRI Fund Weighted Composite Index. However, the average annual standard deviation of the same '40 Act peer group is only about 70 percent of the HFRI peer group, so the average Sharpe ratio for the '40 Act group, at 0.75, is actually slightly better than the average Sharpe ratio for HFRI peer group, at 0.70. A comparison of the year-by-year returns of the two series shows that relatively wide disparities exist between them, with no obvious pattern discernible.

One approach to glean whether a pattern of over- and underperformance may exist is to group the two series by creating five-year rolling periods. Figure 7-4 does this. It presents the average annual rates of return, average standard deviations, and Sharpe ratios for both the HFRI Fund Weighted Composite Index and the '40 Act Alternative Peer Group Index (excluding bear-market funds) for 19 five-year periods from 1990 through 1994 to 2008 through 2012.

FIGURE 7-4   Selected statistics for HFRI and '40 Act alternative peer-group indexes

Five Year Period	HFRI Fund Weighted Composite Index			'40 Act Alternative Peer Group Index Excluding Bear		
	Avg. Annual Rate of Return	Avg. Annual Std. Deviation	Sharpe Ratio	Avg. Annual Rate of Return	Avg. Annual Std. Deviation	Sharpe Ratio
1990–1994	18.00	5.21	2.37	8.87	4.40	0.84
1991–1995	21.96	4.46	3.71	9.93	3.58	1.43
1992–1996	20.33	4.70	3.21	8.88	2.54	1.66
1993–1997	20.24	5.58	2.62	9.30	2.49	1.72
1994–1998	16.13	7.41	1.39	9.23	3.11	1.23
1995–1999	22.35	7.97	2.02	10.58	2.99	1.68
1996–2000	18.25	9.3	1.30	9.33	3.43	1.09
1997–2001	14.36	9.57	0.92	8.46	3.83	0.85
1998–2002	9.54	9.39	0.53	6.62	4.20	0.53
1999–2003	12.15	8.15	1.02	7.49	4.03	0.95
2000–2004	7.34	7.20	0.61	7.38	4.12	1.07
2001–2005	7.61	5.76	0.91	6.92	3.90	1.17
2002–2006	9.26	5.22	1.25	7.64	3.59	1.38
2003–2007	11.87	4.86	1.73	8.59	3.16	1.67
2004–2008	3.74	6.90	0.07	2.83	4.85	–0.08
2005–2009	5.50	7.25	0.34	3.78	5.52	0.14
2006–2010	6.01	7.51	0.48	3.83	5.88	0.25
2007–2011	2.88	7.83	0.20	1.74	6.11	0.07
2008–2012	2.35	7.73	0.25	1.24	6.12	0.14

Sources: Hedge Fund Research, Morningstar, and Forward.

Focusing on the average annual rates of return, this approach tilts the comparison a little more favorably to the HFRI peer-group index. However, when the average annual standard deviations are compared, the '40 Act adjusted peer group is less volatile in every five-year period in the figure. Turning to the Sharpe ratios, the results are split, but the decision goes to the HFRI peer group because the ratios of the hedge funds were higher than the ratios for the '40 Act funds by more than 2:1.

Looking Beneath the Surface: Performance of '40 Act Subsectors

Looking at all these data suggests that no clear winner exists: the performance of the hedge fund group is not obviously superior to the '40 Act funds group and vice versa. Accordingly, let's get more granular in the analysis by comparing certain subsectors of both hedge funds and '40 Act mutual funds with each other. Chapter 2 showed that the investment objectives of hedge funds are currently broader than those of '40 Act alternative mutual funds. Despite U.S. mutual funds having a longer history than hedge funds, a number of hedge fund subsectors operate in markets or have investment policies that are either limited or prohibited by the limitations under which U.S. mutual funds must operate. Recognizing that comparing all hedge funds with all '40 Act alternative funds is therefore a lot like comparing apples to oranges, nevertheless, the performance of the various and more limited '40 Act alternative substrategies can be compared with the performance of specific and appropriate HFRI substrategy indexes.

Equity Long/Short Vehicles

Figure 2-2 showed that equity hedge funds are among the largest substrategies, as measured by both total net assets and the number of hedge funds. Not surprisingly, Figure 3-2 also showed that equity long/short is one of the largest substrategies in the '40 Act alternatives universe.

Moreover, the performance of the '40 Act group can be more directly compared with that of the HFRI equity hedge group. Figure 7-5 shows the annual rates of return over the 23-year period, as well as the average annual rate of return, average annual standard deviation, and Sharpe ratio for each of the series. These data show that

FIGURE 7-5   Annual rates of return and selected statistics for equity long/ short vehicles (1990–2012; monthly data)

Year	HFRI Equity Hedge	'40 Act Alternative Equity Market Neutral
1990	14.43	5.84
1991	40.15	16.56
1992	21.32	9.02
1993	27.94	9.70
1994	2.61	2.40
1995	31.04	16.40
1996	21.75	17.70
1997	23.41	19.96
1998	15.98	19.89
1999	44.22	17.60
2000	9.09	10.87
2001	0.40	4.11
2002	−4.71	−3.20
2003	20.54	18.58
2004	7.68	11.85
2005	10.60	8.66
2006	11.71	9.71
2007	10.48	5.53
2008	−26.65	−17.36
2009	24.57	16.40
2010	10.45	6.45
2011	−8.38	−2.86
2012	7.41	5.06
Avg. Annual Rate of Return	**13.61**	**8.71**
Avg. Annual Std. Dev.	**9.89**	**6.89**
Sharpe Ratio	**0.99**	**0.73**

Sources: Hedge Fund Research, Morningstar, and Forward.

the hedge funds achieved a higher average rate of return, but these vehicles were, on average, almost 50 percent more volatile than the '40 Act alternatives. Moreover, most of the outperformance occurred early in the 1990s, when relatively few '40 Act equity long/short vehicles were operating.

Relative-Value Hedge Funds versus Nontraditional Bond Vehicles

Next, let's compare relative-value hedge funds with the nontraditional bond substrategy of '40 Act alternatives. Figure 7-6 presents the annual rates of return for both series, and the average annual rates of return, average annual standard deviations, and Sharpe ratios for both types of investment companies are also displayed. A comparison of these data show that, once again, the hedge funds recorded returns that were, on average, nearly one-half larger than the returns for the mutual funds, but the data also show that the hedge funds were, on average, more volatile than the '40 Act alternative vehicles.

Comparing the Performance of Market-Neutral Funds

The market-neutral categories for hedge funds and '40 Act alternatives also can be compared directly with each other. Figure 7-7 shows the annual rates of return

FIGURE 7-6   Annual rates of return and selected statistics for relative value hedge funds and nontraditional bond funds (1990–2012; monthly data)

Year	HFRI Relative Value Index	'40 Act Alternative Nontraditional Bond Peer Group Index
1990	13.38	8.37
1991	14.07	18.81
1992	22.26	11.10
1993	27.10	10.17
1994	4.00	1.47
1995	15.66	14.35
1996	14.49	11.98
1997	15.93	11.33
1998	2.81	3.57
1999	14.73	4.56
2000	13.41	4.07
2001	8.92	6.65
2002	5.43	4.60
2003	9.73	14.77
2004	5.58	5.94
2005	6.03	3.17
2006	12.36	6.33
2007	8.94	3.81
2008	−18.03	−11.42
2009	25.81	21.57
2010	11.42	7.02
2011	0.18	0.40
2012	10.59	8.37
Avg. Annual Rate of Return	10.25	7.23
Avg. Annual Standard Deviation	4.39	3.96
Sharpe Ratio	1.49	0.92

Source: Hedge Fund Research, Morningstar, and Forward.

for both hedge funds and '40 Act alternatives, as well as their average annual rates of return, average standard deviations, and Sharpe ratios for the 23-year period from January 1990 through December 2012. A visual inspection of year-to-year returns in this figure shows a fairly close correspondence between the two series. The statistics in the memo items section indicate,

FIGURE 7-7   Annual rates of return and selected statistics for equity market-neutral vehicles (1990–2012; monthly data)

Year	HFRI Market Neutral	'40 Act Alternative Equity Market Neutral
1990	15.45	−2.01
1991	15.65	15.44
1992	8.73	8.76
1993	11.11	14.51
1994	2.65	1.11
1995	16.33	11.92
1996	14.20	7.53
1997	13.62	9.05
1998	8.30	5.28
1999	7.09	8.23
2000	14.56	9.13
2001	6.71	10.07
2002	0.98	4.56
2003	2.44	6.86
2004	4.15	3.47
2005	6.22	3.92
2006	7.32	8.78
2007	5.29	7.61
2008	−5.92	−1.96
2009	1.43	4.22
2010	2.85	0.32
2011	−2.13	1.78
2012	2.98	0.86
Avg. Annual Rate of Return	**13.61**	**5.96**
Avg. Annual Std. Dev.	**9.89**	**3.80**
Sharpe Ratio	**1.03**	**0.63**

Sources: Hedge Fund Research, Morningstar, and Forward.

however, that the average annual rate of return of the hedge fund series is, at 13.61 percent, more than twice the average return for the '40 Act alternative series, at 5.96 percent. However, the data also show that the average annual standard deviation of the HFRI hedge fund series, at 9.89 percent, is more than twice as large as that of the '40 Act peer-group series, at 3.80 percent.

Fund of Hedge Fund Performance versus Multialternative Vehicles

The performance of funds of hedge funds (FoHFs) and multialternative '40 Act funds is probably more imperfect than that of the preceding categories, but the two groups are similar enough to attempt to make the comparison. Figure 7-8 shows the annual performance of the HFRI Fund of Funds Composite Index against

FIGURE 7-8   Annual rates of return and selected statistics for HFRI funds of hedge funds composite and '40 act multialternative funds (2001–2012; monthly data)

Year	HFRI FoHF Composite	'40 Act Alternative
2001	2.80	−10.11
2002	1.02	−23.87
2003	11.61	18.00
2004	6.86	8.84
2005	7.49	4.75
2006	10.39	10.51
2007	10.25	3.83
2008	−21.37	−18.04
2009	11.47	15.66
2010	5.70	6.06
2011	−5.72	−2.57
2012	4.79	3.68
2001–2012		
Avg. Annual Rate of Return	4.25	0.59
Avg. Annual Std. Dev.	5.25	10.00
Sharpe Ratio	0.44	−0.13
2003–2012		
Avg. Annual Rate of Return	4.63	4.60
Avg. Annual Std. Dev.	5.63	6.17
Sharpe Ratio	0.50	0.45

Sources: Hedge Fund Research, Morningstar, and Forward.

the annual performance of the '40 Act Alternatives Multialternative Peer Group Index. The figure begins in 2001 because no multialternative funds existed prior to that time. In addition, only one multialternative fund existed in 2001, and the second and third funds started in late 2002. Accordingly, the first two annual results for the multialternative column should be viewed cautiously because of the category being under-represented. Thereafter, the number of multialternative funds increased, and the HFRI series and the multial-ternative series generally track one another reasonably well. If the first two years of both series are excluded, Figure 7-8 shows that the average annual rate of return for the two series over the 10-year span are 4.63 and 4.60 percent, the average annual standard deviations are 5.63 and 6.17 percent, and the Sharpe ratios are 0.50 and 0.45, respectively. It is clear that the two types of multistrategy vehicles are functionally identical based on these statistics.

Unfortunately, the remaining three types of '40 Act alternative substrategies are not directly comparable for one of three reasons: (1) the '40 Act peer-group perfor-mance record is too short to be a meaningful comparison (managed futures), (2) HFRI does not have a substrategy for currency funds, and/or (3) a large portion of bear-market funds are not directly comparable with HFRI's short-biased substrategy.

Despite the ability to compare each of the '40 Act alternative substrategies with a counterpart using an

HFRI substrategy index, it is reasonable to conclude that (1) the hedge funds appear to generate higher average annual rates of return than the '40 Act alternative vehicles, but they do so with considerably more volatility so that the average Sharpe ratios are relatively indistinguishable from one another. The higher level of risk/volatility for hedge funds is not too surprising because these vehicles operate mostly outside the constraints of the Investment Company Act of 1940 and other federal statutes that mandate a more conservative investment style for mutual fund managers.

8

Active versus Passive Mutual Funds: The Debate Continues

The question of whether active or passive investment management is a superior approach to achieving one's investment goals has been actively debated since the first comprehensive studies of mutual fund performance were published in academic journals. As noted earlier, the pioneers of employing *modern portfolio theory* (MPT) to assess the actual performance of portfolio managers seized on the availability of mutual fund data to construct databases that were used in their analyses.[1] Some of the earliest studies concluded that, as a group, mutual fund portfolio managers underperform broad market equity indexes adjusted for volatility (i.e., risk).[2] This initiated, in turn, a debate about whether mutual fund investors were being amply compensated for the risks and expenses that the portfolio managers were generating to achieve their returns. The initial studies were published in the late 1960s and 1970s, and it is fair to say that the debate has now continued for half a century.[3]

Equity Index Funds Appear on the Scene

It was not just a coincidence that the first index fund was conceived and began operating shortly after the initial quantitative studies of mutual fund performance were published. Most historians cite individuals at Wells Fargo and American National Bank as the first money-management organizations to established index funds in 1973, both based on the Standard and Poor's Composite Index. Both of these funds were created for institutional investors. The prize for the first index mutual fund goes to the Vanguard Group because the firm offered its First Index Investment Trust (later renamed the Vanguard 500 Index Fund) on December 31, 1975. The Vanguard Group was the brainchild of Jack Bogle and was created after he left Wellington Management. Both Vanguard and Bogle are considered to be important representatives of the indexing approach to investing. The underlying thesis of index, or *passive*, investing is that an investor can achieve most of the benefits of allocations to, say, equities without incurring the additional costs of research and portfolio decision making associated with *active* portfolio management. This assumes, of course, that the net effect of these actions and costs detracts from overall returns.

The addition of index mutual funds as an investment alternative to potential investors changed the debate from a theoretical basis to one of investment reality. Mutual fund investors now had the opportunity to allocate all or a portion of their investable funds to products that, by and large, carried lower total expenses than actively managed funds. Equity index funds initially were confined to well-known, broad-based equity indexes, such as the Standard & Poor's 500 Index (S&P 500), but the success of the early products spawned a proliferation of index mutual funds in which investment-management companies began using less well-known and narrower indexes as well as fixed-income indexes as the basis for the mutual fund's investment objective.

Are Index Funds Truly Passive?

It's worth asking the question: Are index funds truly passive? Index funds, whether they are mutual funds or exchange-traded funds (ETFs), are managed by investment managers with an investment objective of replicating the performance of an index of a specific financial market (such as the S&P 500 for larger-capitalization U.S. equities). The goal of most financial-market indexes is to encapsulate all the prices in a defined market for a defined period of time and to then measure the change from one defined period to another defined period.

Readers will recall from Chapter 3 that one of the first U.S. stock-market indexes was the Dow Jones Industrial Average (DJIA) created by *Wall Street Journal* editor and Dow Jones & Company cofounder Charles Dow. It was created on February 16, 1885, and it represented the U.S. dollar average of the stock prices for 14 companies: 12 railroads and 2 industrial companies. On May 26, 1896, a group of 12 U.S. industrial stocks were chosen by Dow, and perhaps others, to comprise the DJIA, and this list was eventually expanded to 30 "industrial" companies. Dow had previously created the Dow Jones Transportation Average (July 3, 1884), and the indexes were used by Dow to create his Dow theory of stock-price movements, a strategy that originated from a large number of his editorials in the *Wall Street Journal.*

The DJIA is a *price-weighted* index in that it was originally calculated by summing the 30 stock prices of the companies comprising the index and dividing the sum by 30. However, once stock splits and stock dividends began occurring, the index's divisor had to be reduced, and it is currently less than 1.0. Charles Dow's goal in creating the index was to establish a measure of the overall value of the U.S. stock market and its changes over any defined period: one minute, one hour, one month, and so forth. The components of the DJIA eventually were decided by a committee of senior editors at Dow Jones & Company, and the group dropped the "industrial-only" restriction many years ago. Nevertheless, the goal of the committee was to create an index that regularly reflected the overall value of U.S. (large-cap) stocks over time.

Standard & Poor's (S&P), a division of McGraw Hill Financial, now owns the DJIA, and senior representatives of the company are charged with maintaining the DJIA Index. Standard & Poor's also has a long history of creating indexes. It introduced its first U.S. stock-price index in 1923, but the S&P 500 was first published on March 4, 1957. Both the DJIA and the S&P 500 are comprised of companies that are selected by a committee, although the S&P stock price index is a free-float, capitalization-weighted stock price index. The goals of both indexes are nearly identical: to capture the level and movement of (largely) U.S.-domiciled corporations that are generally the largest companies with shares offered to the general public.

Whereas the underlying methodologies of both the DJIA and the S&P 500 have important differences, it is important to remember that both indexes represent the methodologies that reflect the ultimate goal of the groups charged with creating and maintaining the indexes. Therefore, an index fund based on the S&P 500 implicitly assumes that an investor wants to allocate his or her capital based on the premise that the largest (mostly) U.S. companies represent the best way to have an allocation to U.S. equities. The index fund investor is relying on the Standard & Poor's committee to make any periodic changes in the composition of the index such that it will always reflect the characteristics that the committee is trying to achieve (these characteristics include market capitalization, liquidity, domicile, public float, sector classification, financial viability, and others). In addition, the index fund investor is relying on the fund's investment advisor to employ an investment strategy that will replicate the underlying index as closely as possible (i.e., with a minimal level of tracking error).

As index funds have become more prolific, a number of investment advisors have created index funds that offer investment strategies that are different from that employed by a fund based on the S&P 500. Examples of different index techniques include, but are not limited to, equal weighting of stocks or weighting based on a company's total revenues rather than total market capitalization.

The most recent *Investment Company Institute (ICI) Fact Book* pegs the total net assets of index mutual funds at $1,312.0 billion, and this is comprised of 373 vehicles. Figure 8-1 indicates that equities account for nearly 80 percent of the total, and ICI data indicate that more than 41 percent of the equity total reflects S&P 500 index fund net assets.

Investors seeking indexed strategies have another avenue to pursue in addition to traditional index funds. Chapter 3 indicated that the first ETF was introduced on the American Stock Exchange in January 1993. Known as S&P Depository Receipts (SPDRs) or *Spiders*, the vehicles were initially limited to passively managed index funds, but in 2008, the Securities and Exchange

FIGURE 8-1 Total net assets and number of equity versus hybrid and bond mutual funds (billions of dollars)

	Net Assets			Number		
Year-end	Total	Equity	Hybrid and Bond	Total	Equity	Hybrid and Bond
1993	27.4	24.0	3.4	69	59	10
1994	32.1	28.2	3.9	81	66	15
1995	57.0	51.0	6.0	87	73	14
1996	97.8	89.3	8.5	105	89	16
1997	170.3	156.4	13.9	132	111	21
1998	265.0	244.8	20.2	156	138	18
1999	387.4	361.1	26.3	197	176	21
2000	384.0	357.1	26.9	271	245	26
2001	370.6	334.2	36.4	286	260	26
2002	327.4	281.4	46.0	313	284	29
2003	455.3	404.4	50.9	321	292	29
2004	554.0	493.8	60.2	328	301	27
2005	618.7	548.2	70.5	322	295	27
2006	747.5	664.7	82.8	342	316	26
2007	854.7	748.2	106.5	354	322	32
2008	601.7	481.1	120.6	359	337	32
2009	835.4	677.6	157.8	357	314	43
2010	1016.7	824.1	192.6	365	323	42
2011	1094.3	855.8	238.5	383	338	45
2012	1312.0	1030.5	281.5	373	327	46

Source: Investment Company Institute Fact Book 2013.

Commission (SEC) began to authorize the creation of actively managed vehicles. Because the SEC limited ETFs to index vehicles for 15 years, the overwhelming majority of the total net assets and the number of ETFs are, not surprisingly, index funds. Figure 8-2 shows that nearly all the total net assets of ETFs are in vehicles that have an investment mandate to replicate the investment performance of an index. At year-end 2012, for example, more than 90 percent of ETF net assets were being managed with index mandates, with about half this amount

FIGURE 8-2   Net assets and number of ETF '40 Act investment companies (billions of dollars). Data prior to 1993 are unavailable

Year-end	Net Assets			Number		
	Total	Index	All Other	Total	Index	All Other
1993	464	464	–	1	1	–
1994	424	424	–	1	1	–
1995	1,052	1,052	–	2	2	–
1996	2,411	2,411	–	19	19	–
1997	6,707	6,707	–	19	19	–
1998	15,568	15,568	–	29	29	–
1999	33,873	33,873	–	30	30	–
2000	65,585	65,585	–	80	80	–
2001	82,993	82,993	–	102	102	–
2002	1,02,143	1,02,143	–	113	113	–
2003	1,50,983	1,50,983	–	119	119	–
2004	2,27,540	2,26,205	1,335	152	151	1
2005	3,00,820	2,96,022	4,798	204	201	3
2006	4,22,550	4,07,851	14,699	359	343	16
2007	6,08,422	5,79,516	28,906	629	601	28
2008	5,31,288	4,95,560	35,728	728	670	58
2009	7,77,128	7,02,600	74,528	797	727	70
2010	9,91,989	8,90,908	1,01,081	923	844	79
2011	10,48,134	9,38,958	1,09,176	1,134	1,028	106
2012	13,37,112	12,17,096	1,20,016	1,194	1,071	123

Source: Investment Company Institute Fact Book 2013.

in U.S. broad-based or sector indexes. The remaining ETFs were either actively managed mandates or non–Investment Company Act of 1940 (non–'40 Act) ETFs, which consist primarily of commodities, currencies, and futures.

Figures 8-1 and 8-2 indicate that the overwhelming number of both index funds and ETFs is based on investment mandates where each fund's investment advisor is offering a product mandated to replicate an index, and most of these indexes are equity based, with the S&P 500 commanding the largest share. Focusing

FIGURE 8-3   Total net assets and number of index mutual funds and index ETFs (billions of dollars). Data prior to 1993 are unavailable

Year-end	Net Assets				Number			
	'40 Act Industry Total	Total	Index Mutual Funds	Index ETFs	'40 Act Industry Total	Total	Index Mutual Funds	Index ETFs
1993	2,070.0	27.9	27.4	0.5	4,534	70	69	1
1994	2,155.3	28.6	28.2	0.4	5,325	82	81	1
1995	2,811.3	52.1	51.0	1.1	5,725	89	87	2
1996	3,525.8	91.7	89.3	2.4	6,248	124	105	19
1997	4,468.2	163.1	156.4	6.7	6,684	141	132	19
1998	5,525.2	260.4	244.8	15.6	7,314	185	156	29
1999	6,846.3	395.0	361.1	33.9	7,791	227	197	30
2000	6,964.6	422.7	357.1	65.6	8,155	351	271	80
2001	6,974.9	417.2	334.2	83.0	8,305	388	286	102
2002	6,383.5	383.5	281.4	102.1	8,243	426	313	113
2003	7,204.2	555.4	404.4	151.0	8,125	440	321	119
2004	8,095.1	720.0	493.8	226.2	8,040	479	328	151
2005	8,891.1	844.2	548.2	296.0	7,974	523	322	201
2006	10,397.9	1,072.6	664.7	407.9	8,118	685	342	343
2007	12,001.5	1,327.7	748.2	579.5	8,026	955	354	601
2008	9,603.7	976.7	481.1	495.6	8,022	1,029	359	670
2009	11,113.0	1,380.2	677.6	702.6	7,663	1,084	357	727
2010	11,831.9	1,715.0	824.1	890.9	7,555	1,209	365	844
2011	11,627.4	1,794.8	855.8	939.0	7,591	1,411	383	1,028
2012	13,045.2	2,247.6	1,030.5	1,217.1	7,596	1,444	373	1,071

Source: Investment Company Institute Fact Book 2013.

on the index totals for both types of vehicles, Figure 8-3 presents both the net assets and the number of funds for index mutual funds and index ETFs from year-end 1993 through 2012. These data demonstrate the remarkable growth of index mutual funds and the even more remarkable growth of index ETFs. Summing the two types of vehicles shows that they had a total net worth of $27.9 billion at year-end 1993 with 70 vehicles. Figure 8-3 also presents the ICI's total net assets and the number of funds for all investment companies, which at year-end

1993 stood at $2,070.0 trillion and 7,596 vehicles, respectively. Therefore, index-mandated investment companies accounted for 1.4 percent of the industry's net assets and 1.5 percent of the number of funds. At the end of the decade, December 31, 1999, the index fund share of the industry's total net assets rose to 5.8 percent, and the number of vehicles was 2.9 percent.

Although the overall level of stock-price gains was well below their longer-run average over the first decade of the new millennium, index mutual funds and index ETFs continued to grow rapidly. Figure 8-3 shows that by year-end 2009, the total net assets of the two types of index vehicles rose to $1,380.2 billion, and the number of vehicles stood at 1,084. At these totals, they represented 12.4 percent of industry assets and 14.2 percent of the number of vehicles. The figure also shows that the overwhelming proportion of this growth can be attributed to index ETFs. Three factors probably account for both the strong overall growth of index products and the accelerated success of ETF vehicles. First, many investors grew increasingly disenchanted with the MPT of fund investing that had dominated financial markets for the previous two decades. Style Box asset-allocation schemes proved to be a poor answer for investors when, as in 2008, most financial asset prices tumbled and correlation coefficients rose appreciably. Second, market researchers improved and expanded the use of indexes for fixed-income vehicles, and this created a much broader and deeper market for ETFs (and bond index mutual funds) than in earlier years. Third, fund investors became much more aware of the management fees and operating expenses of traditional mutual funds, and many investors and their investment advisors began touting lower-cost index vehicles for a portion of each investor's asset allocation.

Performance Bias against Large-Cap Funds

The debate between active and passive strategies focused, from the outset, on large-cap mutual funds and broadly based stock-price indexes of large-cap companies. Much of the discussion in academia has focused on the *efficient-market hypothesis*, an assertion that highly efficient markets are informationally efficient such that stock prices impound all available information. If this is the case, a portfolio manager cannot consistently achieve returns above average market returns on a risk-adjusted basis. There are, of course, a very large number of assumptions imbedded in this statement, and relaxing or testing of these assumptions has sparked a very active debate for several decades.

Most academicians assert that there are three forms of the efficient-market hypothesis: (1) the *strong* form claiming that financial-asset prices trading in liquid two-way markets instantly reflect both public and nonpublic information in prices, (2) the *semistrong* form asserting that stock prices reflect all publically available information and change almost instantly to impound this information in prices, and (3) the *weak* form claiming that prices on traded assets (stocks and bonds) already reflect all publically available information. A corollary of the weak form is that excess returns cannot be earned in the long run by using investment techniques based only on historical share prices. However, we saw in Chapter 6 that a very large number of commodity trading advisors (CTAs) employ only an analysis of historical prices, and the longer-run results of many of these programs appear contrary to the weak form of the efficient-market hypothesis.

This is an interesting topic, but it is beyond the scope of this undertaking to either review all the literature or definitely conclude whether financial markets are or are not efficient. However, it is worth examining the topic of whether actively managed mutual funds are or are not superior to passively managed funds in greater detail.

As noted earlier, most of the literature comparing active and passive strategies focuses on funds that invest mainly in large-capitalization stocks and use as their performance benchmark a broadly based index of large-cap (mostly) U.S. stocks such as the S&P 500. This is not surprising, of course, because these companies are the most widely held by U.S. investors. However, we also know that the U.S. mutual fund industry is currently comprised of more than 7,500 mutual funds, and only a portion of these vehicles focuses on U.S. large-cap stocks to achieve their investment objectives. Many of these funds focus on niche categories, such as small-cap companies, and certain sectors of the myriad investment companies that focus on companies domiciled outside the United States.

Active versus Passive: Comparing Apples to Apples

The argument that passive investment strategies produce superior results to active strategies rests largely on the idea that the higher costs of active strategies erode results such that passive strategies earn the investor a higher rate of return, all other things being equal. It can be and has been easily demonstrated that passive strategies focusing on large-cap U.S. stocks have lower management fees and expense ratios than actively managed funds focusing on similar stocks. Therefore, if these actively managed funds are unable to earn enough excess return (i.e., alpha) to offset the fees and expenses generated in their investment process, then, on average, passive investment funds may be a superior way to achieve one's investment objective.

But is this always the case? Most investors elect to hold a variety of stocks and funds in their portfolios. Therefore, looking only at large-cap funds in the active versus passive debate is overly simplistic because most investors are attempting to achieve resilient, all-weather portfolios, and these typically include specialized asset classes and strategies. In other words, investment vehicles that may be appropriate at managing exposure in large-cap, highly liquid sectors may not be the ones that investors should look to when constructing a well-diversified portfolio.

To answer this broader question, Forward Management constructed a study of annual mutual fund returns over the past 20 years. The goal was to see whether a very wide variety of actively managed vehicles produced superior or inferior investment results versus index funds and/or index ETFs after all fees were taken into account. Forward Management used Morningstar data for the analysis. It assembled asset classes that included all U.S. stock, international stock, sector stock, and taxable bond categories for those groups that had at least five years of investment returns and also had at least five years of index fund returns. Therefore, the analysis included each year for which performance results were available from December 31, 1992, through December 31, 2012. The study used the institutional share class for each of the actively managed and index funds, and if multiple institutional share classes existed, then the share class with the longest track record was used.[4] In all, 30 asset classes were created with a minimum of five years of performance data and a maximum of 20 years of performance data.

The results of this study show that actively managed funds outperform index funds in 16 of the 30 categories examined. These results are presented in Figure 8-4. The 30 asset classes are quite diverse; they range from large-cap growth, large-cap blend, and large-cap value to sector classes such as healthcare, real estate, and diversified Pacific/Asia. The asset classes also include fixed-income strategies such as long-term bond and long government. A perusal of the asset classes in Figure 8-4 suggests that passively managed index funds posted better investment results than actively managed funds in the asset classes that operated mostly in relatively efficient

FIGURE 8-4 Average annual returns between actively managed and index funds (December 31, 1992–December 31, 2012; monthly data)

Morningstar Asset Class	Proportion of Months Active Outperformed Passive	Average Performance Difference
Consumer Defensive	75.0	2.4
Health	75.0	4.2
Industrials	75.0	3.2
Europe Stock	70.0	1.7
Real Estate	68.8	0.9
Small Cap Value	64.3	1.0
Financial	62.5	4.4
Utilities	62.5	1.1
Diversified Pacific Asia	60.0	5.0
Foreign Large Cap Blend	60.0	0.7
Foreign Large Cap Value	60.0	−0.9
Small Cap Blend	55.0	1.6
Communications	50.0	−0.2
Intermediate-Term Bond	50.0	0.0
Long-Term Bond	50.0	−1.0
Large Cap Growth	50.0	0.9
Intermediate-Term Government	45.0	0.0
Mid Cap Blend	45.0	0.2
Diversified Emerging Markets	44.4	1.0
Long-Term Government	40.0	−3.1
Large Cap Blend	40.0	−0.4
Short-term Bond	38.9	−0.6
Consumer Cyclical	37.5	−1.4
Energy	37.5	1.1
Technology	37.5	0.6
Large Cap Value	35.0	−0.4
Mid-Cap Growth	30.0	−0.9
Mid-Cap Value	30.0	−1.0
Natural Resources	25.0	2.2
Small Cap Growth	14.3	0.2
Average	**49.6**	**1.6**

Source: Forward.

financial markets such as large cap, mid cap, and sectors dominated by larger companies such as communications and consumer cyclical companies. However, actively managed funds outperformed passive funds in a slight majority of asset classes (16 of 30), and these asset classes were predominately more niche asset classes such as healthcare, small-cap blend, real estate, and other classes.

In addition to the previous figure, Figure 8-4 also presents the difference in average annual returns between actively managed vehicles and index funds. These data more clearly show the asset classes where active investment management outperforms index funds. Looking at the data in this manner produced superior returns, some sizable, in many of the sector-specific, international and domestic small-cap categories. Passive strategies, on the other hand, outperformed in the domestic large-cap equity and many of the bond fund categories.

These data, while certainly not conclusive, strongly suggest that the widely held school of thought (expounded ad nauseam by indexing proponents) that the performance of index funds is superior to actively managed vehicles is a more complicated topic than generally believed. Index funds have a role in the asset-allocation decision in many portfolios. However, actively managed funds also have an important role. As investors attempt to build portfolios that will achieve their investment goals, they probably should consider both active and passive funds in their attempt to construct resilient, all-weather portfolios.

The active versus passive debate also can be analyzed by estimating the average annual returns, annual volatilities, and Sharpe ratios for each of the asset categories on a vehicle-by-vehicle basis with the same population of actively managed and passive index funds that are shown in Figure 8-4. These data are summarized in Figure 8-5.

FIGURE 8-5   Selected performance measures of active and passive funds (December 31, 1992–December 31, 2012)

| Asset Class Morningstar Category | Active Minus Passive Difference | | |
	Average Annual Rate of Return	Annual Standard Deviation	Sharpe Ratio
Short-Term Bond	−0.70	0.08	0.29
Utilities	0.79	0.08	0.29
Industrials	3.23	1.58	0.27
Intermediate-Term Government	−0.38	−0.88	0.26
Financial	3.18	−1.51	0.15
U.S. Long-Term Bond	−1.02	−0.89	0.15
Consumer Defensive	2.38	4.06	0.15
Consumer Cyclical	−1.58	−1.15	0.14
Large Cap Blend	−0.12	−0.07	0.11
Diversified Pacific Asia	4.03	1.83	0.07
Mid Cap Value	0.22	2.26	0.05
Long-Term Government	−2.23	−5.81	0.04
Diversified Emerging Markets	−0.09	0.14	0.03
Communications	−0.14	2.49	0.03
Mid-Cap Growth	−0.63	−0.08	−0.02
Health	1.48	0.94	−0.05
Intermediate-Term Bond	−0.07	0.53	−0.08
Large Cap Value	−0.35	−0.71	−0.09
Natural Resources	2.02	2.60	−0.15
Small Cap Blend	1.47	0.30	−0.16
Large Cap Growth	0.53	0.92	−0.18
Real Estate	0.66	1.67	−0.19
Technology	0.16	0.45	−0.23
Small Cap Growth	−0.69	3.08	−0.23
European Stock	0.85	1.32	−0.24
Small Cap Value	0.35	0.71	−0.27
Energy	0.08	−6.90	−0.30
Foreign Large Cap Blend	1.15	0.23	−0.31
Mid Cap Blend	−0.33	2.26	−0.34
Foreign Large Cap Value	0.27	3.77	−0.58

Source: Forward.

Figure 8-5 presents these statistics as differences between the average active results and the passive, or index, results. Sixteen of the Morningstar asset-class categories show higher average annual rates of return, 21 display higher average annual volatility, and 14 show higher Sharpe ratios. All these results are after the deduction of all the expenses to offer the product, so these data support the same conclusion that was demonstrated in Figure 8-4. Actively managed mutual funds appear to outperform passive index funds about half the time, so the widely held assertion that index mutual funds or ETFs are a superior way to achieve one's investment goals is not borne out by quantitative results.

9

Role of Asset Allocation

Most investors are well aware that some of the largest university endowment funds have achieved long-run performance that has been very meritorious. These institutions have been leaders in adopting diversified multi-asset-class portfolios that have earned relatively high average annual rates of return with moderate levels of risk. The chief investment officer of the Yale endowment, David F. Swensen, and the Yale's Investment Committee have adopted, for example, an alternative investment approach to achieving the goals of Yale University that has contributed to sustaining the university as a global leader in higher education.[1] Over the two-decade span ending June 30, 2012, the university's 20-year returns were a market-leading 13.7 percent per annum, producing $17.3 billion in additional relative value to support Yale's mission of teaching and research.

Yale has been joined by Harvard University and other leading schools of higher education in using the tools of modern portfolio theory (MPT) to allocate their investable assets to a wide variety of asset classes. Allocating only a small amount of investable assets to traditional U.S. equities and bonds and more to alternative investments is known as the *endowment model of investing*. The endowment model allocates a significant portion of assets to nontraditional asset classes such as absolute return, private equity, and real estate. Endowments, foundations, ultra-high-net-worth investors, and family offices typically believe that less-liquid assets provide a good source of excess returns. At the same time, many of these investors have an unlimited, or close to unlimited, time horizon that allows them to bear the liquidity risk of such investments. One need only look at the average asset allocations of Yale and Harvard over the 2001–2012 period, as shown in Figure 9-1, to gauge the power of having these types of investments in an asset allocation.[2]

FIGURE 9-1   Average annual asset allocation of Harvard and Yale Universities (fiscal year-end; percentages)

Period	Global Equities	Global Fixed Income	Real Estate	Commodities	Hedge Fund	Managed Futures	Private Equity
2001	35	18	9	6	7	7	18
2002	31	21	7	6	6	6	21
2003	35	20	8	8	7	7	14
2004	34	19	6	11	9	9	12
2005	34	18	6	11	9	9	12
2006	34	17	6	12	9	9	11
2007	32	15	9	13	10	10	11
2008	34	13	11	11	9	9	13
2009	31	14	13	10	9	9	14
2010	26	9	13	11	11	11	19
2011	20	13	13	12	10	10	21
2012 e	19	17	11	10	11	11	21

Sources: Frontier Investment Management 2001–2011; 2012 estimated by author.

Reviewing the investment strategies of U.S. colleges and universities is relevant to all investors because these investors have consistently achieved superior rates of return with moderate levels of risk. Consequently, it may not be possible to achieve the same returns and volatilities as the major endowment investors, but adopting the same investment techniques and asset classifications will allow smaller investors to improve their long-run returns.

Bringing the Endowment Model to the Mass-Affluent Investor

As we have seen in previous chapters, the blend of alternative investment strategies with the transparency, liquidity, and the regulatory structure of retail investment vehicles has growing appeal to both financial advisors and investors. These investors, just like the endowments, foundations, ultra-high-net-worth individuals, and family offices, desire diversification and noncorrelated returns.

The pursuit of noncorrelated returns is one of the principal tenets of asset allocation. Asset allocation involves determining which mix of asset to hold in a portfolio. The choices are seemingly infinite, but each investor must determine, or have it determined for him or her, the asset allocation that appears to have the best chance of achieving that investor's investment goals. Two fundamental factors that will contribute to each individual investor's asset allocation are *time horizon* and *tolerance for risk*. Neither of these factors is static, easily measured, or known with certainty. Time horizon seems relatively straightforward, but the ultimate goal of the investor (paying for one's children's higher education, amassing wealth for a comfortable retirement, or some other goal) cannot be determined with complete certainty. Likewise, risk tolerance is an elusive concept that can change with one's economic circumstances, age, and a whole host of other variables. Regardless of the difficulty of determining these factors, any choices made about determining an investor's mix of assets results in an asset allocation.

Types of Asset-Allocation Models

Many researchers divide asset-allocation strategies into broad groups such as strategic asset allocation, tactical asset allocation, and core-satellite asset allocation. *Strategic asset allocation* attempts to create an asset mix that will provide an optimal balance between expected return and risk (typically measured as the standard deviation of return) for a longer-term horizon. *Tactical asset allocation* is usually a more active strategy by an investor that shifts the allocations between asset classes in a manner that will, hopefully, be additive to the investor's long-run rate of return. Finally, *core-satellite asset allocation* is a combination of the previous two asset-allocation strategies.

Asset allocation relies on the notion that different asset classes offer return streams that are not perfectly correlated, and this, as we know from previous chapters, is the fundamental benefit of diversification. Chapter 4 noted, for example, that the correlation between the Hedge Fund Research Indices (HFRI) Fund Weighted Composite, the Standard & Poor's 500 Index (S&P 500), and the Barclays Aggregate U.S. Bond Index is relatively low and negative, respectively, so that the amount of the HFRI allocation, given its strong risk-adjusted track record, dominated the three-asset portfolio.

Rather than relying, however, on a peer-group index that reflects all manner of hedge funds, let's try adding an equal allocation from peer-group indexes for, say, three different hedge fund substrategies and constraining the allocations to 5 and 10 percent each for the three substrategies. To add a degree of reality to the exercise, the three hedge fund subindexes will be the HFRI Equity Hedge (Total) Index, the HFRI Macro: Systematic Diversified Index, and the HFRI ED: Merger Arbitrage Index. Why these three? The underlying reasoning is that (1) equity long/short (as reflected by the HFRI Equity Hedge Index) reflects one of the largest portions of the alternative investment universe, (2) managed futures are widely understood and available (as reflected by the HFRI Macro: Systematic Diversified Index), and (3) merger arbitrage is a relatively straightforward event-driven strategy. To begin the exercise, Figure 9-2 shows the average annual rates of return, annual volatilities, and Sharpe ratios for each of the five assets that will be in the portfolio. In addition, the figure also shows

FIGURE 9-2   Selected statistics for certain indexes (January 1990–December 2012; monthly data)

Index	Average Annual Rate of Return	Annual Standard Deviation	Sharpe Ratio	Correlation Coefficient				
				(1)	(2)	(3)	(4)	(5)
(1) S&P 500	8.55%	15.01%	0.33	1.00	0.12	0.74	0.42	0.52
(2) Barclays Aggregate	6.90%	3.70%	0.90	0.12	1.00	0.05	0.07	0.10
(3) HFRI Equity Hedge	13.61%	9.89%	0.99	0.74	0.05	1.00	0.51	0.57
(4) HFRI Macro: Sys. Diversified	11.32%	7.85%	0.97	0.41	0.07	0.51	1.00	0.28
(5) HFRI ED: Merger Arbitrage	9.19%	4.56%	1.21	0.52	0.10	0.57	0.28	1.00

Sources: Hedge Fund Research, Morningstar, and Forward.

the correlation matrix for each index. These data show that the average annual rates of return, annual volatilities, and Sharpe ratios are higher, in some cases appreciably so, for the three HFRI substrategy indexes than the S&P 500 and the Barclays Aggregate. Moreover, the correlation matrix shows that the correlation coefficients for the three substrategy indexes are relatively low vis-à-vis the S&P 500 and nearly uncorrelated with the Barclays Aggregate. Therefore, if we simply optimized using the five assets, the result would be quite similar to the results in Chapter 4: the hedge fund substrategies would dominate the S&P 500 and result in a fairly small allocation to the Barclays Aggregate. However, the data span the entire 23-year period from January 1990 through December 2012, and, in a manner similar to the discussion in Chapter 4, it is highly unlikely that a typical investor would have had the foresight to allocate a large portion of his or her available assets to the then relatively unknown asset substrategies in January 1990.

FIGURE 9-3   Average annual rates of return, annual standard deviation, and Sharpe ratios for selected indexes and portfolios (January 1990– December 2012; monthly data)

Index/Portfolio	Average Annual Rate of Return	Annual Standard Deviation	Sharpe Ratio
S&P 500	8.55%	15.01%	0.33
Barclay's Capital Aggregate Bond	6.90%	3.70%	0.90
60% S&P 500: 40% Barcap Aggregate	8.33%	9.16%	0.51
52.5% S&P 500: 32.5% Barcap Aggregate: 5% HFRI Equity Hedge: 5% HFRI Macro: Sys.: 5% HFRI ED-Merger	8.73%	8.79%	0.58
45% S&P 500: 25% Barcap Aggregate: 10% HFRI Equity Hedge: 10% HFRI Macro: Sys.: 10% HFRI ED-Merger	9.27%	8.32%	0.67

Sources: Hedge Fund Research, Morningstar, and Forward.

In a more realistic scenario, let's assume that the investor starts in January 1990 with a 60:40 allocation of stocks (as measured by the S&P 500) to bonds (as measured by the Barclays Capital U.S. Aggregate Bond Index). The third row of Figure 9-3 presents the average annual rate of return, annual standard deviation, and the Sharpe ratio for the portfolio over the entire 23-year period from January 1990 through December 2012. Next, let's add 15 percent, divided equally in the amount of 5 percent each, of each of the three hedge fund index substrategies, as represented by the HFRI Equity Hedge Index, the HFRI Macro: Systematic Diversified Index, and the HFRI ED: Merger Arbitrage Index. The fourth row of Figure 9-3 presents the results. Not surprisingly, the addition of an alternative investment sleeve, even at only 15 percent of the total allocation, boosted the average annual return to 8.73 percent and pared the annual standard deviation to 8.79 percent. Together these items produced a Sharpe ratio for the portfolio of 0.58. Also not surprising are the portfolio statistics when the alternative sleeve doubles to a 10 percent allocation into each of the three hedge fund substrategies. The fifth row of Figure 9-3 shows that the average annual rate of return moves up to 9.27 percent, the annual standard deviation is 8.32 percent, and the Sharpe ratio climbs to 0.67. Rows 4 and 5 demonstrate that adding a relatively small amount of alternative investment substrategies can have a large impact on a portfolio's outcome.

What Is Due Diligence?

Due diligence is a commonly used term in financial markets, but what exactly does it mean? The *Merriam-Webster Dictionary* gives two definitions of the term: "(1) the care that a reasonable person exercises to avoid harm to other persons or their property and (2) research and analysis of a company or organization done in preparation for a business transaction (as a corporate merger or purchase of securities)." The second definition is more applicable when it comes to researching a particular company or investment fund as a possible candidate for inclusion in a portfolio. The term came into common use as a result of the Securities Act of 1933, when it called for a "due diligence defense" to actions by a broker-dealer when it was accused of inadequate disclosure to investors of material information with respect to the purchase of securities.

Accordingly, investment firms do various amounts of due diligence when they propose either a financial transaction such as a merger between two firms or the inclusion of an investment company in a portfolio. Investment advisors charging a fee for their services may be required to defend their due-diligence practices if the investment proves to be unsuitable for an investor's financial objectives or if the investment fails to perform because it was not managing the strategy in an appropriate and prudent manner.

In the case of hedge funds, the relative lack of a federal regulatory structure for many of their activities makes due diligence an important aspect of their marketing activities. It is usually divided into two aspects: investment due diligence and operational due diligence. *Investment due diligence* is a review of the hedge fund's investment strategy, objectives, and controls. The key document is the fund's offering memorandum, where the general partner states what the strategy is attempting to achieve, how it is going to be achieved, and what controls are in place to assure limited partners that the strategy will be rigorously adhered to. *Operational due diligence* is less "sexy" than investment due diligence, but it is at least as important, or perhaps more so, as investment due diligence. More often than not, the hedge fund "blowups" that appear on the front pages of financial publications can be traced to some aspect of the hedge fund's operations rather than its investment strategy. Operational due diligence is wider than just back-office concerns.

It includes such areas as technology and systems, business continuity and disaster-recovery programs, legal and compliance issues, regulatory risk, compensation and employee turnover, service providers, counterparty oversight, and a host of others.[3]

Academicians and other market researchers have not focused much on asset-allocation techniques and their impact on returns in recent years. One seminal study was published by Brinson, Hood, and Beebower in 1986. The authors substituted appropriate indexes for the major allocations of a large number of pension funds, and the indexed returns were shown to be higher than the pension plans' actual returns over the 10-year period ending in 1983.[4] Brinson, Singer, and Beebower published a follow-up article in 1991, and taking these findings together, many researchers have concluded that asset allocation is a much more important determinant of portfolio returns than security selection over time.[5] More recent studies have pointed out that explaining a high proportion of a portfolio's variance, as the Brinson et al. studies do, does not fully explain a portfolio's performance.

Introducing Smart Beta Index Funds: Is It Active Management in Disguise?

Chapter 8 showed that the passive money-management techniques may be appropriate for highly efficient markets but that active portfolio management can be superior in less-efficient markets. From the standpoint of asset allocation, this suggests that index mutual funds and index exchange-traded funds (ETFs) may be appropriate vehicles for large-capitalization allocations but that actively managed vehicles are the correct choice in markets, both debt and equity, that are characterized by inefficiency. A relatively recent entrant into these debates is the so-called smart beta vehicles. *Smart beta* is an umbrella term for rules-based investment strategies that do not use the conventional market-capitalization weights. Smart beta strategies attempt to deliver a better risk and return tradeoff than conventional market-cap-weighted indices by using alternative weighting schemes based on measures such as volatility or dividends. A number of studies are available that purport to demonstrate that market-weighted capitalization schemes, those used by most index mutual funds and index ETFs, can be outperformed by weighting schemes that employ various fundamental characteristics such as book value, sales, dividends, and cash flow.

It is important to recognize that these smart beta schemes carry operating costs that are above those of the bargain-basement index mutual funds and index ETFs. This is not too surprising when one remembers that all index strategies have an underlying premise in their construction and that smart beta indexes have a strategy that likely requires more frequent changes than the more traditional capitalization-weighted indexes.

It's probably too soon to make a judgment on smart beta index vehicles, but the idea of using them in a portfolio with capitalization-weighted index vehicles and actively managed vehicles is appealing. This is an area that will likely witness a lot of product development over the next few years, and investors will want to follow these developments closely.

Risk Budgeting: Panacea or Placebo?

Risk budgeting is a portfolio management technique that is used widely by institutional investors. Simply stated, it is a technique that allows an investor to regularly assess the risks associated with a portfolio of assets and to plan on how much risk one is willing to assume with any given mix. It is important to realize, however, that these risks are not static and that an investor's ability to assume risk is also variable. Target-date funds are an easy and simple way of risk budgeting. An investment-management company offering a target-date-fund product sets a target date for an investor based on, say, his or her expected retirement date. The product is designed to allocate to riskier investments in the earlier years and then shift to a more conservative asset allocation as the investor approaches retirement.

The critical element to understand is that the risk level associated with any given portfolio changes over time and that these changes need to be tracked and managed. Risk budgeting can be broken down into three steps. First, establish a target risk level for your portfolio. Second, estimate the total portfolio risk of the assets, and build a portfolio that matches your target risk. Finally, manage the portfolio to maintain the risk level close to the target level. All this may sound relatively simple, but implementing such a plan can be very time-consuming. Nevertheless, the most important facet of risk budgeting is to consider the overall risks that you are able to bear, build a portfolio that reflects those attributes, and regularly evaluate where you are and what you are trying to achieve.

10

Assessing Liquid Alternative Expense Ratios

Early chapters of this book made the point that the overwhelming majority of hedge funds carry fee arrangements that are a management fee of 2 percent plus a performance fee of 20 percent with a high-water mark. A less well-known feature of hedge funds, and certainly not emphasized by hedge fund managers or general partners, is that limited partners also pay a variety of other expenses as well. There are no existing academic studies documenting the amount of these fees, but industry professionals probably agree that these fees can amount to as much as 1 percent per year. Thus, assuming that the hedge fund manager makes a gain for limited partners in any year (and the agreement has no hurdle rate), it is common for the limited partners to pay annual fees of as much as 5 percent. Few hedge fund investors have a problem paying these relatively steep fees when returns are consistently high (between, say, 10 and 15 percent), but recent years have produced much lower returns for both equity- and debt-oriented investments. Thus management and other fees are now playing an increasingly important role in the allocation decisions of all types of investors.

Are Exchange-Traded Fund Expense Ratios as Low as Popularly Perceived?

Let's begin by examining the expenses of exchange-traded funds (ETFs) because most investors perceive them to be quite low. As with any registered investment company, ETF investors pay a variety of fees when they purchase the vehicles as part of their portfolio allocation. Many ETF sponsors emphasize that the typical ETF, the overwhelming majority of which are index vehicles, is cheaper than an actively managed mutual fund or other investment vehicle because ETF organizations incur relatively low expenses to license the underlying index from an index provider plus the cost of creating the vehicle for investors. Most investors are aware that ETFs are exchange-traded instruments, and each ETF therefore has a bid-ask spread. Arbitrage can keep many of these spreads at a low level, but it is not uncommon for ETFs to sell at a premium or a discount to their net asset value. And there are brokerage-fee commissions to be paid on each trade, so anyone other than infrequent ETF traders will need to assess these costs as well. The largest, and most well-known, ETFs are based on the Standard & Poor's 500 Index (S&P 500), and these vehicles have the lowest expense ratios.

Understanding Expense Ratios

An *expense ratio* is a measure of what it costs to operate a registered investment company, and the ratio is commonly expressed as a percentage of net assets. The largest portion of an actively managed vehicle's expense ratio is typically the management fee, and this is the cost that the investor adviser charges the mutual fund to manage the portfolio on an ongoing basis. This expense will be for the portfolio manager and the manager's team, plus the all-in costs of research on the underlying securities. In addition, the mutual fund will have fund administration charges, daily fund accounting and pricing fees, shareholder services expenses, distribution charges (known as *12b-1 fees*), director fees, and other miscellaneous expenses. These expenses are typically paid on a daily basis, and because many portfolios generate steady income from dividend payments or coupon payments, the expenses are netted out from the income flow. All registered investment companies are required to publish their expenses on an annual basis, and these data are in the prospectus and the vehicle's annual report.

The *2013 Investment Company Institute (ICI) Fact Book* states that the 2012 average *asset-weighted* expense ratio for funds with an equity-oriented investment objective was 0.77 percent (or 77 basis points) versus a non-asset-weighted average of 1.41 percent, and the average for bond-oriented funds was 0.61 percent (or 61 basis points) versus a non-asset-weighted ratio of 1.01 percent. In both cases, it should be noted, the average expense ratios for actively managed funds were considerably higher than those for index funds.

Figure 10-1 shows the average expense ratios for 16 different ETF strategies grouped into three broad asset classes: equity, fixed income, and specialty. In all, expense ratios are shown for 1,193 ETF vehicles. Not surprisingly, the U.S. large-capitalization asset class, represented by

FIGURE 10-1   ETF expense ratios by selected strategies (expense data in basis points)

Asset Class	Strategy Focus	Number of ETFs	ETF Data Expense Ratios (bps) Average	Low	High
Equity	U.S. Large Cap	86	16.57	4	60
Equity	U.S. Non-large Cap	64	31.41	10	70
Equity	U.S. Sectors	154	45.09	14	148
Equity	Global & International	157	50.39	12	159
Equity	Emerging Markets	127	67.06	18	98
Fixed Income	Government, NGA, Corporate, Mortgage	70	37.86	5	173
Fixed Income	High Yield	11	62.08	30	145
Fixed Income	Inflation Protection	12	27.08	7	50
Fixed Income	International	29	57.06	25	65
Fixed Income	Municipal	32	35.88	20	167
Specialty	Dividend/Fundamental	90	52.33	7	113
Specialty	Inverse/Leveraged	177	99.98	71	269
Specialty	Preferred, Target Date, Etc.	112	68.89	15	232
Specialty	International	42	75.17	20	254
Specialty	Commodity	44	76.34	25	166
Specialty	Currency	22	50.28	40	75
Total		**1,193**	**59.75**	**4**	**269**

Sources: State Street ETF Industry Guide, March 28, 2013, and author's groupings.

86 ETF vehicles, posted an average expense ratio, on an equal-weighted basis, of 16.57 basis points, with the lowest fee at 4 basis points and the highest fee at 60 basis points. The figure also shows that the average expense ratios for other equity asset classes are considerably higher than the average for the U.S. large-cap category. U.S. non-large-cap ETFs have an average expense ratio of 31.41 basis points, and U.S. sector ETFs show an average of 45.09 basis points. Global and international equity-market ETFs offered to U.S. investors have a still larger average expense ratio, 50.39 basis points (with a high of 159 basis points), and emerging-markets ETFs have an average expense ratio of 67.06 basis points.

Moving to the fixed-income asset class, the five subcategories have average expense ratios that range from 27.08 basis points (inflation protection) to 62.08 basis points (high yield). And in a manner similar to the equity asset classes, the range spans from a low of 7 basis points to a high of 173 basis points. Also presented in Figure 10-1 are six specialty subcategory asset classes ranging from dividend/fundamental-focused to currency-focused ETFs. All these substrategies have average expense ratios of more than 50 basis points, with the inverse/leveraged category averaging 99.98 basis points. Several of the substrategies also have some vehicles posting high expense ratios in the neighborhood of 250 basis points.

In all, the 1,193 ETFs have an average expense ratio, not weighted by assets under management, of 59.75 basis points. One should couple this with an estimate of brokerage fees and the possibility of buying above the net asset value or selling below the net asset value. This results in all-in fees that are likely below the average expense ratios for actively managed funds but higher than the commonly perceived view that ETFs are "much" cheaper than mutual funds.

Decomposing Mutual Fund Expense Ratios

As mentioned earlier, the *2013 Investment Company Institute (ICI) Fact Book* states that the average expense ratio for a non-asset-weighted, actively managed equity mutual fund was 141 basis points in 2012, whereas the ratio for a bond fund was 101 basis points. Unfortunately, the ICI does not disaggregate the data into its various components, so another data source must be used. Fortunately, other mutual fund groups collect these data and make them available to industry professional and others. Figure 10-2 presents these data, which were sourced from Strategic Insights. The figure presents four "gross" fee columns that sum to each mutual fund's gross fee, and all the data are presented as a percentage of average net assets for the fund's most recent year. The four fee categories are

1. *Gross advisor fee.* This is the fund-level gross investment advisory fee expressed as a percentage of average assets for the latest reporting period.
2. *Gross administrative fee.* A mutual fund's administrator handles the many back-office functions for

FIGURE 10-2 Average assets and expense ratios for selected mutual fund asset classes

Mutual Fund Asset Class	Avg. Assets ($MM)	Total Net Fee	Gross				
			Total Fee	Advisor Fee	Admin Fee	Operating Fee	Dist./Mtg. Fee
U.S. Stock (n = 1242)	$2,161	0.882	1.150	0.683	0.141	0.377	0.098
Sector Stock (n = 211)	$1,157	1.046	1.251	0.734	0.119	0.459	0.063
Balanced (n = 211)	$455	0.921	1.315	0.703	0.198	0.489	0.101
International Stock (n = 599)	$1,686	1.094	1.614	0.826	0.166	0.687	0.096
Commoditites (n = 18)	$2,746	0.851	1.260	0.763	0.134	0.462	n/a
Taxable Bond (n = 747)	$2,735	0.635	0.763	0.472	0.099	0.224	0.105
Tax-Exempt Bond (n = 279)	$1,065	0.566	0.620	0.424	0.088	0.153	0.070
Total: Non-Alternative (n = 3,307)	$1,942	0.856	1.139	0.658	0.135	0.405	0.089
Alternative (n = 124)	$406	1.600	2.255	1.261	0.212	0.848	0.052
Total (n = 3,431)	$1,887	0.949	1.279	0.733	0.145	0.460	0.083

Sources: Strategic Insights and Forward.

a fund. These include clerical and fund account-ing services, data processing, bookkeeping, and internal auditing, as well as preparing and filing Security and Exchange Commission (SEC), tax, shareholder, and other reports.

3. *Gross operating fee.* This is a general category that includes the costs of printing and mailing reports, trustee fees, and all other fees that are not advi-sory, administrative, or 12b-1-related.

4. *Gross distribution/marketing fee.* A 12-b-1 fee is used for distribution costs such as advertising and commissions paid to distributors.

These four fee categories are summed to arrive at each mutual fund's *gross total fee.* However, the second column of data in Figure 10-2 indicates that the average total fee is usually above the average net total fee. This reflects the fact that many mutual fund management companies will elect to execute waiver or reimbursement agreements with the fund's adviser or other service providers, espe-cially when a fund is new and expenses tend to be higher (due to a small asset base). The management company will agree to these waivers to reduce expenses to some pre-determined level or by some predetermined amount. In some instances, these waiver amounts can be repaid over a period that generally cannot exceed three years from the year in which the original expense was incurred.

Turning to the first row of data in Figure 10-2, 1,242 mutual funds whose investment objective focuses on

U.S. stocks posted a total fee of 0.882 percent. As a group, these types of funds had an average gross fee of 1.150 percent, so the managers elected to waive 0.233 percent in this year. Reading across the row, advisory fees constitute nearly three-fifths of the average fund's total expenses, with operating expenses being the second-largest category.

Figure 10-2 presents data for eight mutual fund asset categories. The figure shows that average expense ratios are somewhat lower for fixed-income funds (both taxable and tax-exempt), and this reflects lower advisory fees and, to a lesser extent, lower administrative and operating fees. The figure also shows that U.S. mutual funds focusing on international markets have higher advisory and operating fees than do funds focusing on domestic markets. Somewhat surprisingly, the commodity fund category does not display fees that are significantly different from those of the other categories, although this largely reflects the fact that one commodity-oriented mutual fund, the PIMCO Total Real Return Fund, accounts for almost half the category's total net assets.

The figure also shows data for the nonalternative categories versus the averages for the 125 mutual funds that employ alternative strategies. These data show the total fee ratio for nonalternative mutual funds at 0.856 percent versus a total fee ratio of 1.600 percent for the alternative strategy funds. Looking at the gross fee categories shows the same pattern. The average gross advisor fee for the alternative mutual funds is 1.261 percent versus

0.658 percent for the nonalternative funds, and the gross administrative fee and gross operating fee are appreciably higher as well. Some of the higher expense ratios for the alternative category likely reflect the smaller average size of the mutual fund category. These are, of course, newer mutual funds, and it is commonplace for relatively new and/or smaller assets under management (AUM) funds to have expenses that are relatively large. This appears to be borne out by the average expense waiver for the category as well. Figure 10-2 shows that the average total fee for the alternative category is 1.600 percent, whereas the gross total fee averages 2.255 percent, a difference of 0.655 percent.

Are Liquid Alternative Expense Ratios Too High?

In light of the evidence shown in Figure 10-2, it is reasonable to ask whether alternative mutual fund expense ratios are too high. This chapter has shown that ETF and other index mutual funds have the lowest expense ratios, although they are higher than commonly perceived by most investors. This chapter also has shown that fixed-income mutual funds have lower expense ratios than equity-oriented funds and that non-U.S.-focused investment strategies are higher still. Nevertheless, Figure 10-2 demonstrates that recent expense-ratio data show that Investment Company Act of 1940 ('40 Act) alternative mutual funds have relatively high expense ratios. However, investors must recognize that the expense ratios of these liquid alternatives are, on average, well below the expenses incurred by hedge fund and other alternative investment partnerships. Whether the liquid alternatives fees are too high ultimately will depend on whether the funds deliver on their performance objectives for their shareholders. It is also likely that these fees will move lower as time passes and more vehicles enter the marketplace and existing funds accumulate more net assets.

11

Getting Started

Let's begin this final chapter with a review of what this book has covered. It began with a brief overview of the early days of the mutual fund industry and showed how a relatively small industry eventually grew to become the largest single investment force in the U.S. capital markets. Next, the early days of the hedge fund industry were documented, with the discussion emphasizing that their focus on ultra-high-net-worth individuals, family offices, endowments, and foundations grew out of the statutory limitations of U.S. security laws. This was followed by a contrasting of the structural, marketing, and operational differences between limited-partnership hedge fund vehicles and Investment Company Act of 1940 ('40 Act) vehicles. Once again, most of these differences reflect the U.S. regulatory structure, especially the stricter limitations on investment companies that are fully subject to the regulations of the Investment Company Act of 1940.

Building on the premise that '40 Act alternative vehicles are registered investment companies pursuing hedge fund strategies as a mutual fund or exchange-traded fund (ETF), the book reviewed the various sub-strategies of hedge funds and '40 Act alternative vehicles with an emphasis on how portfolio managers attempt to make money for their investors. We learned, for example, that the remuneration arrangement of most hedge funds (a 2 percent annual management fee and a 20 percent performance fee with a high-water mark) rewards portfolio managers who achieve acceptable returns with minimal drawdowns. This strategy focus is commonly associated with an *absolute-return focus*, but this, while laudatory, was not borne out in most hedge fund returns in the "great recession" of 2007–2008. This section also discussed the strong case for adding alternative vehicles to a portfolio to achieve more efficient long-run results.

Chapter 5 reviewed the performance history of hedge funds from January 1990 through December 2012. Hedge fund performance results were extraordinarily strong over most of the 1990s, and hedge funds performed meritoriously in the first few years of the new millennium, even as broadly based U.S. equity indexes put up three consecutive calendar years of negative performance. However, the "great recession" has proven to be a sea change for hedge fund performance: as capital-market returns have shifted lower, the "2 and 20" hedge fund model is increasingly viewed by investors as too rich for investment managers. Moreover, aggregate hedge fund returns, as measured by the peer-group indexes of

Hedge Fund Research and others, are generally trailing long-only vehicles, so many high-net-worth investors, family offices, pension funds, endowments, and others are looking to allocate to vehicles that offer acceptable returns and volatility at lower fees.

Managed futures constitute an asset strategy that has a long history, but it is always surprising to me how little many investors know about managed futures. Accordingly, an entire chapter was devoted to the history of commodity trading advisors (CTAs), their regulatory structure, performance, and portfolio attributes, and the relatively short-lived entrance of '40 Act managed futures vehicles as candidates for allocation in an alternatives portfolio. The performance of both CTAs and '40 Act managed futures vehicles has been lackluster over the last few years, but a strong case still can be made for adding at least one managed futures vehicle to a portfolio for its history of maintaining low correlation with stock and bond returns over longer periods.

Although the terms '40 Act alternatives or liquid alternatives have come into the financial lexicon only in the last seven or eight years, evidence was presented in the early chapters that many of the mutual funds now categorized by Morningstar, Statistical Insights, and others have existed for many years. However, a legitimate question could be asked about the overall performance characteristics of '40 Act alternative mutual funds. This questioned was answered by creating peer-group sub-strategies of liquid alternatives for the 23-year period spanning 1990–2012. The early years had relatively few vehicles, but just like the early days of both mutual funds and hedge funds, more and more vehicles were created by investment-management companies, and the complexity and breadth of the offerings grew steadily. Moreover, once the bear-market category was eliminated from the overall results, the remaining six substrategies, individually and as a group, performed extremely well. Whereas it is true that head-to-head performance comparisons of hedge fund peer groups with '40 Act alternative peer groups showed that the returns of hedge funds were, on average, above those of liquid alternative vehicles, the hedge funds were also considerably more volatile than the '40 Act vehicles, and their Sharpe ratios were quite similar.

One vexing issue that has been debated almost continuously since the early studies were published on risk-adjusted performance of mutual funds is whether, as a group, actively managed mutual funds outperform or underperform index funds. A large number of academicians and certain other researchers have concluded that large-capitalization index funds offer superior performance, after all fees are taken into account, than mutual funds that have investment objectives focusing on large-cap companies. However, when the analysis is broadened to include mutual funds that operate in asset classes less efficient than large-cap, mostly non-U.S. stocks, such as emerging markets and small-cap funds, the evidence presented suggests that, on average, actively managed funds offer slightly better performance than index funds. This same chapter also pointed out that all indexes have a construction strategy embedded in them so that a capitalization-weighted index fund of larger mostly U.S. companies, such as a Standard & Poor's 500 Index (S&P 500) fund, is not a "purely" passive strategy, and many of the so-called smart beta index fund strategies are really just another method of semi-systematic investing. The book also discussed some of the various ways that asset allocation techniques have been employed to contribute to the debate about active portfolio management.

This was followed by a discussion of mutual fund expenses. This section showed that mutual fund and ETF expenses are a function of the investment strategy and focus of the investment manager. In the case of ETFs, the evidence showed that U.S. large-cap index funds had by far the lowest expense ratios but that the expense ratios of other strategies were considerably higher than those of these well-known vehicles. With regard to '40 Act alternative funds, the average expense ratio in 2012 was 1.65 percent versus 0.89 percent for non-'40 Act alternative vehicles. The expense data confirmed that the largest difference between active and passive strategies is the management-fee remuneration, and the data also showed that the difference between '40 Act alternatives and other actively managed vehicles is higher management fees and other operating expenses for the liquid alternatives funds.

Thus, bringing all the information presented in this book into the calculus of structuring an all-weather portfolio for the typical investor, how should one get started in the process? The first step is to make a complete and honest review of one's historical track record. For individuals who have all or most of their investable assets with one broker-dealer or other financial institution, this should not be too difficult a task. However, most investors have their investable assets in at least two and perhaps many more institutions, so the task is more daunting. There are, of course, a number of financial apps and other devices that allow differently sourced portfolios to be aggregated, and some financial firms will accommodate their clients by aggregating assets held away from the firm.

Once a reasonably accurate track record is established, each investor needs to take a hard look at his or her record with an eye toward identifying patterns or systematic tendencies that are causing the results to be less than desired. Many financial firms have individuals trained to assist investors with this task, and as in seeking medical advice, it never hurts to get a second opinion.

Five years have now elapsed since the meltdown of the "great recession." Equity valuations have recovered some, or all, of the decline, and U.S. home prices appear to have bottomed out and are rising broadly. Using this information, how has your portfolio of investable assets performed? Are you adequately diversified? Does your portfolio have too heavy a tilt toward fixed-income assets?

Are you beginning to reach an age where the income component of your portfolio will need to be relied on to supplement your day-to-day living expenses? Would you like to make a career change that focuses more on personal fulfillment than on maximizing income? All these are important questions, and structuring your investable assets and other assets (such as the equity in your home) will play an important role in each investor's future happiness.

Using '40 Act alternatives in your investment portfolio is, in all likelihood, part of the answer to constructing and maintaining an all-weather portfolio. However, it is unlikely that these investment vehicles will provide most investors with all the answers. This book has demonstrated that investors must take a broader view of the investment landscape to achieve their investment goals. Thirty or forty years ago, the vast majority of the investing public had brokers or other financial advisors that helped them to pick portfolios of stocks and bonds. As time passed, the investing public shifted a larger portion of their portfolios to professional money managers such as mutual funds. And, as time passed, more and more companies moved away from defined-benefit pension plans to defined-contribution plans that placed the burden of selecting retirement-oriented investments to the plan participant. Mutual funds, investment banks, commercial banks, insurance companies, and other intermediaries stepped into this void and tailored products to meet the needs of these new asset allocators.

The financial markets also *globalized*, and investors began to look at investment options that held assets domiciled in non-U.S. developed markets, emerging markets, and even frontier markets. Thus the choices today are intimidating in both the numbers and the information needed to make good decisions.

Should investors devote a portion of their assets to directly owning stocks and bonds? The answer is probably "yes," but individual investors need an *edge*, which probably means access to a financial advisor with access to information and products that meet the longer-run needs of the client. Should investors allocate a portion of their investable assets to index funds and ETFs? The answer again is probably "yes," but the overall objective should be a core component to one's overall portfolio. Should investors avail themselves of '40 Act alternative or liquid alternatives vehicles? Once again, the answer is "yes," but the investor should be looking for strategies that allow his or her overall portfolio risk to be managed to an acceptable level, and some of these strategies probably need to focus on markets or investment strategies that have a specific role in achieving an all-weather portfolio.

Most investors probably should attempt to have 20 to 30 percent of their portfolios devoted to liquid alternative strategies.[1] Global returns are likely to be lower over the next 10 to 20 years than they were over the late 1990s, and the phenomenal 30-year bull market in fixed-income vehicles is likely behind us. Somewhat lower returns and heightened volatility are conditions that make alternative investments increasingly important going forward, and '40 Act vehicles give investors unique strategies, full transparency, daily liquidity, and the protection of regulatory standards that will help investors to achieve their financial goals.

Endnotes

Chapter 1

1. Matthew P. Fink, *The Rise of Mutual Funds* (New York: Oxford University Press, 2008). According to Fink, the first mutual fund was the Massachusetts Investors Trust, which was started on March 21, 1924.

2. Some researchers dispute whether the Jones model was the first hedge fund. These authors point out that the idea of combining short positions with long positions predated Jones's fund and that arbitrage techniques also had been employed by portfolio managers for many years prior to the Jones hedge fund.

3. Alfred Winslow Jones, "Fashions in Forecasting." *Fortune* March 1949: 88–91, 180, 182, 184, 186. A. W. Jones received public acclaim for his investing skill when he was featured in a 1966 *Fortune* article authored by Carol Loomis entitled, "The Jones Nobody Keeps Up With." Loomis went on to have a long professional relationship with investor Warren Buffett, contributing to his now-famous Berkshire Hathaway annual chairman letters. She authored a book in 2012 about Buffett entitled, *Tap Dancing to Work*.

4. Investment Company Institute, *Investment Company Fact Book: 2010* (Washington, DC: Investment Company Institute, 2007).

5. This suggests that the average mutual fund account was about $3,500.

6. Barry Eichengreen and Donald Mathieson, "Hedge Funds: What Do We Really Know?" *Economic Issues No. 19*, International Monetary Fund, Washington, DC, September 1999.

7. Michael Steinhardt started Steinhardt Partners in 1967 (originally called Steinhardt, Fine and Berkowitz) with coinvestors William Salomon (former managing partner of Salomon Brothers) and Jack Nash (who later formed Odyssey Partners with Leon Levy). The fund eventually closed, distributing all monies to its limited partners, in 1995, after outperforming the S&P 500, after fees, by triple the amount of the index's gain over the same period.

8. Soros eventually received an enormous amount of notoriety when his principal hedge fund, the Quantum Fund, sold short more than $10 billion in British pounds in September 1992. This was in reaction to the U.K. government's refusing to either raise short-term interest rates to levels that were comparable with those of other European exchange-rate mechanisms countries or to allow the value of the British pound to float in foreign-exchange markets. The U.K. government eventually withdrew from the mechanism and devalued the British pound, and the Quantum Fund is estimated to have earned over $1.1 billion.

9. A recently published study by Citi Prime Finance, "The Rise of Liquid Alternatives and the Changing Dynamics of Alternative Product Manufacturing and Distribution," May 2013, predicts, among other things, that total net assets of liquid alternatives will reach $1.7 trillion by December 31, 2017.

Chapter 2

1. Securities and Exchange Commission, "Implications of the Growth of Hedge Funds," Washington, DC, September 2007.

2. FINRA was formed by a consolidation of the enforcement arm of the New York Stock Exchange (NYSE), NYSE Regulation, Inc., and the National Association of Security Dealers (NASD). The merger was approved by the SEC on July 26, 2007.

3. It is commonplace for mutual funds to encounter pricing issues on some issues, and most fund managers have an

operations department to work at arriving at a fair price for each security. This has become a more difficult task with the globalization of security markets with different time zones, security laws, and foreign-exchange values.

Chapter 3

1. Any universe of companies or investment companies that spans a reasonable length of time is subject to *survival bias*. This means that the results over time may be better than actually achieved because the companies that "failed to survive" drop out of the universe. Almost any index is subject to some degree of survivorship bias. This includes broad stock indexes such as the Dow Jones Industrial Average (DJIA) or the Standard & Poor's 500 Index (S&P 500), as well as the peer-group indexes of hedge fund index providers.

2. This description is excerpted from the Caldwell & Orkin website. Active management of the Caldwell & Orkin Market Opportunity Fund commenced on August 24, 1992. A prior fund passively managed and indexed to the largest 100 over-the-counter (OTC) stocks began operations on March 11, 1991. The fund initiated the use of short selling on May 2, 1994.

3. "Caldwell & Orkin Market Opportunity Fund: Investment Process," Caldwell & Orkin Funds, Inc., Norcross, GA.

4. The Gabelli ABC Fund has achieved an average annual rate of return of 6.42 percent since inception. The investment manager does not use the S&P 500 as either its primary or its secondary benchmark. Instead, the fact sheet lists the Lipper U.S. Treasury Money Market Average as the primary benchmark, and it lists the S&P Long-Only Merger Arbitrage Index as the secondary benchmark.

5. Long Term Capital Management, L.P., was founded in 1994 by John W. Meriwether, former vice chairman and head of bond trading at Salomon Brothers. Members of LTCM's board of directors included Myron S. Scholes and Robert C. Merton, who shared the 1997 Nobel Prize in economic sciences. LTCM used strategies combined with very high financial leverage. The firm's master fund collapsed in 1998, leading to an agreement,

on September 23, 1998, among 14 financial institutions for a $3.6 billion recapitalization (bailout) under the supervision of the Federal Reserve. A lot has been written about LTCM, and most of the analyses point to the firm's high leverage as the cause of the collapse. The Russian ruble currency crisis was a precipitating cause of LTCM's meltdown, and the initial leverage of the vehicle, described to be 10:1 or even as high as 20:1, rose dramatically as its equity shrank with losses.

6. The Series 31 test is also available for those who wish to receive trailing commissions on commodity limited partnerships, commodity pools, or managed accounts guided by commodity trading advisors. The Series 31 license is also meant for those supervising these same limited activities. However, individuals who take this exam in lieu of the Series 3 exam cannot open individual futures trading accounts. A prerequisite is a FINRA registration, usually the Series 7 exam.

Chapter 4

1. The Barclays Capital Aggregate Bond Index is a broad-base index maintained by Barclays Capital, which took over the index business of the now-defunct Lehman Brothers, and is used to represent investment-grade bonds being traded in the United States.

2. There are, of course, myriad ways to manage the portfolio. One example would be to rebalance the portfolio every year-end to a 60:40 ratio at the beginning of each year. Doing so in this example would result in a slightly improved average annual return and higher Sharpe ratio than the single 60:40 allocation over the period.

Chapter 6

1. The removal of counterparty risk means that all contract specifications are guaranteed by the clearinghouse, typically composed of Futures Commission merchants (FCMs). However, as many commodity market participants have learned in recent years, the clearinghouse guarantee does not extend to the relationship between the FCM and its clients.

2. Richard L. Sandor and Norman E. Mains, "Futures Markets," in Edward I Altman (ed.), *Handbook of Financial Markets and Institutions*, 6th ed. (New York: Wiley, 1987).

3. The economic rationale for cash-settled futures contracts is that the underlying market on which the futures contract is based is sufficiently liquid and deep that no individual or group can meaningfully influence the outcome. Thirty years after the initiation of Eurodollar futures contract trading, the thesis is being questioned by individuals at several financial institutions who admit that they participated in gaming the polling process so that the outcome was distorted.

4. In listing futures contracts on new goods, instruments, or indexes, it is important to be the *first mover*. Once liquidity is established in a contract, it is difficult to dislodge the frontrunner. In the case of stock-index futures, the CBOT elected to place its bet on a futures contract using the Dow Jones Industrial Average (DJIA). However, the publisher of the DJIA, Dow Jones & Company, decided that it did not want its index to be used as the basis for a futures contract. The CBOT ignored the request of Dow Jones to cease and desist, arguing that the DJIA was in the public domain, but Dow Jones & Company eventually prevailed in court. The CBOT tried other stock-index contracts, but the CME's lead was too large to overcome.

5. BarclayHedge, as of December 31, 2011.

6. Scott H. Irwin and Cheol-Ho Park, "What Do We know about the Profitability of Technical Analysis?" *Journal of Economic Surveys* 21(4):786–826, 2007.

7. Galen Burghardt, Ryan Duncan, and Lianyan Lin, "Two Benchmarks for Momentum Trading," AlternativeEdge Research Note, Newedge Prime Brokerage, Chicago, August 26, 2010.

8. Andrew Lo, Harry Mamaysky, and Jiang Wang, "Foundations of Technical Analysis: Computational Algorithms, Statistical Inference and Empirical Implementation." *Journal of Finance* 55(4):1705–1761, 2000.

9. John Lintner, "The Potential Role of Managed Commodity-Financial Futures Accounts in Portfolios of Stocks and Bonds,"

presented at the Annual Conference of the Financial Analysts Federation, Toronto, Canada, May, 1983.
10. Harry M. Kat, "Managed Futures and Hedge Funds: A Match Made in Heaven," *Journal of Investment Management* 2(1): 32–40, 2004.
11. Ibbotson Associates, "Managed Futures and Asset Allocation," Chicago, February 25, 2005.
12. Edward Szado, "VIX Futures and Options: A Case Study of Portfolio Diversification during the 2008 Financial Crisis." *Journal of Alternative Investments* 12(2):68–85, 2009.
13. Morningstar, *Managed-Futures Category Handbook*, Chicago, 2011.

Chapter 7

1. Forward Asset Management's quantitative investments team published two of these studies: Nathan Rowader, "The 10 Percent Problem," Forward Thinking-Viewpoint, Ridgefield, NJ, 2013; and Nathan Rowader, "The 5 Percent Problem: Double Jeopardy for Traditional Bond Investors," Forward Thinking-Viewpoint, Ridgefield, NJ, 2013.

Chapter 8

1. The earliest articles focusing on mutual fund performance were written by Jack L. Treynor, John Lintner, and William F. Sharpe. See Jack L. Treynor, "How to Rate the Management of Investment Funds." *Harvard Business Review* 43(1):63–75, 1965; Jack L. Treynor and Kay Mazuy, "Can Mutual Funds Outguess the Market?" *Harvard Business Review* 44:131–136, 1966; John Lintner, "Mutual Fund Performance." *Journal of Business* 1966; and William F. Sharpe, "Mutual Fund Performance." *Journal of Business* 39(2):119–138, 1966.
2. Michael C. Jensen, "Risk, the Pricing of Capital Assets, and the Evaluation of Investment Portfolios." *Journal of Business* 42(2):167–247, 1969; this was an influential study focusing on mutual fund performance. I challenged Jensen's overall empirical conclusion (that mutual fund portfolio managers, as a group, underperformed the Standard & Poor's 500 Index

(S&P 500) adjusted for risk, in "Risk, the Pricing of Capital Assets, and the Evaluation of Investment Portfolios: Comment." *Journal of Business* 50(3):371–384, 1977.

3. Burton G. Malkiel, *A Random Walk Down Wall Street* (New York: W. W. Norton, 1973). This book is now in its eleventh edition. Malkiel argues that asset prices typically exhibit signs of a random walk and that one cannot consistently outperform market averages. The book is frequently cited by those who favor the efficient-market hypothesis. Malkiel suggests that given the distribution of fund performances, it is statistically unlikely that an average investor would happen to select those few mutual funds that will outperform his or her benchmark index over the long term.

4. Forward's methodology included ETFs and the performance of liquidated investment companies but excluded fund of funds results and enhanced index fund results.

Chapter 9

1. David F. Swensen, *Pioneering Portfolio Management: An Unconventional Approach to Institutional Investment* (New York: Free Press, 2000).

2. Frontier Investment Management, "Investing Like the Harvard and Yale Endowment Funds," Dallas, TX, April 2012.

3. Jason A. Scharfman, *Hedge Fund Operational Due Diligence: Understanding the Risks* (Hoboken, NJ: Wiley, 2009).

4. G. P. Brinson, R. Hood, and G. L. Beebower, "Determinants of Portfolio Performance." *Financial Analysts Journal* 42(4): 39–44, 1986.

5. G. P. Brinson, D. D. Singer, and G. L. Beebower, "Determinants of Portfolio Performance. II: An Update." *Financial Analysts Journal* 47(3):40–48, 1991.

Chapter 11

1. Hari P. Krishnan and Norman E. Mains, "A Quantitative Model for Asset Allocations to Hedge Funds," *Wilmott Magazine*, July–August 2004, 87–91.

Index

About the Author

Norman E. Mains, PhD is a Managing Director at Forward, a San Francisco-based money management firm that offers mutual funds, separately managed accounts and hedge funds. Norman is the head of the New Products Committee and the Chief Risk Officer at Forward. Prior to joining Forward, he was the chief investment officer and director of research at Graystone, a group wholly owned by Morgan Stanley that focused on creating customized funds of hedge funds for ultra high net worth individuals, family offices, endowments, and foundations. Prior to this position, Norman worked for a large French bank running their offshore fund of hedge fund business, a position that he took after being the chief economist and director of research at the Chicago Mercantile Exchange. Norman worked for three broker/dealers in Chicago and Los Angeles earlier in his career, one of which was Drexel Burnham Lambert where he worked with the founder of the interest rate futures market. Norman moved to Chicago from Washington, DC, where he was a senior economist for the Federal Reserve Board after being employed by the mutual fund industry's trade association, the Investment Company Institute. Norman was awarded his PhD from the University of Warwick in England. He now lives in Napa, CA, with his wife, Ginna.